PRAEGER CLASSICS IN POLITICAL SCIENCE

What is the Third Estate?

EMMANUEL JOSEPH
SIEYÈS

What is the Third Estate?

TRANSLATED BY M. BLONDEL
AND EDITED, WITH HISTORICAL NOTES, BY
S. E. FINER

INTRODUCTION BY
PETER CAMPBELL

FREDERICK A. PRAEGER, *PUBLISHERS*
NEW YORK · WASHINGTON · LONDON

FREDERICK A. PRAEGER, *Publishers*
111 Fourth Avenue, New York 3, N.Y., U.S.A.
77–79 Charlotte Street, London W.1, England

Published in the United States of America in 1964
by Frederick A. Praeger, Inc., Publishers

Printed in Great Britain

Contents

What is the Third Estate? is one of the very many books that are far more talked about than read. As anybody who reads the work will see, this is a great pity, but the fact itself is hardly surprising. The last French edition, 1888, is today an exceedingly rare book, while no English translation appears ever to have been made at all—unless, that is, we are to credit the highly problematical existence of a purported translation of 1791, of which, in any event, no copies seem to be extant.

It is precisely to make Sieyès's cutting and immensely influential classic available to the English-speaking world that the present edition has been prepared.

In the translated version, Sieyès's italics have been retained, but not his use of capital letters. This was as erratic as it was lavish, and it has been thought best to simplify and to standardise it. Again, in the original texts Sieyès's own notes appear at the foot of the page. Placed in that position these interesting, pungent but often lengthy notes prove most distracting to the reader, and so, in this edition, they have been identified in the text by a letter of the alphabet and relegated to a position succeeding the main body of the text.

Sieyès's work ran through four editions in 1789, and in some minor respects these differ from one another. In this version the *variorum* readings are given at the foot of the page in which they occur.

To explain some of Sieyès's contemporary allusions, a short chronological summary and brief historical notes have been added.

The *Introductory Essay* of my friend and colleague Professor Peter Campbell, of the University of Reading, opens this version of *What is the Third Estate?* with a clear and incisive analysis of the personality of Sieyès and the permanent elements in his political thought.

S. E. FINER

SIEYÈS AND *WHAT IS THE THIRD ESTATE?*

by Peter Campbell

The man

In 1789 Sieyès heralded the start of the French Revolution; in 1799 he presided over its end. *Qu'est ce que le Tiers Etat?* summoned the populace to assert its rights and to assume control of the national destiny. Its author was never the leader of the Revolution but both as a propagandist and as a politician he played an important part in its development. In this book and in other writings he provided not only the agenda for the Revolution in France but also the themes for popular movements in the nineteenth and twentieth centuries, for he expressed with passion and clarity the principles of popular sovereignty, national unity and social equality.

Sieyès* might be regarded either as a member

* According to J. H. Clapham, *The Abbé Sieyès*, Westminster, 1912, p. 1, f.n. 1, 'He signed his own name Sieyès, Sieyés, or Sieyes.' According to G. G. van Deusen,

3

of the class that was to make the Revolution and
benefit from it or as one of the class-traitors who
so often lead revolutionary or reactionary movements. Born (in 1748) into a bourgeois family of
noble origins and of moderate prosperity (his
father had independent means and was also a tax
inspector), he was educated at schools conducted
by the Jesuits and the Doctrinaires and became a
priest. As a seminarist and as a young priest he
was more interested in philosophy and music
than in the doctrines of the Church. Chief among
the authors whom he read were Bonnet, with his
notions of the natural order and harmony of
things, Condillac, with his ideas on the contrac-
tual nature of government, on the advantages of
representative government, and on the evil of inequality, and Locke, with his views on the people
as the ultimate sovereign, on representation, and
on majority rule. These and other writers had a
profound influence on Sieyès, although he had
too independent a mind for it to be said that he
was anybody's disciple.

In 1775, Sieyès became secretary to Mgr. de
Lubersac, Bishop of Treguier, who became
Bishop of Chartres in 1780. Sieyès went with him
and became vicar-general and, ultimately, a

Sieyes: his life and his nationalism, New York, 1932, p. 11,
f.n. 1, Camille Desmoulins recorded that the name was
pronounced 'Syess'.

canon and chancellor of the diocese. In 1787 the King convoked Provincial Assemblies. As a representative of the clergy in the assembly of his province Sieyès seems to have been an influential participant in an unsuccessful experiment. In the same year he advised the *Parlement* of Paris, then exiled to Troyes, to force the arrest and execution of the minister responsible for its exile. He became a member of the Lodge of the Nine Sisters, to which Condorcet, Danton, and Desmoulins belonged, and he became associated with the circle of the Duke of Orléans.

In August 1788, the King summoned the States-General of the kingdom to meet in May 1789. Sieyès set himself to declare what were the needs of France and the means of satisfying them. In four pamphlets he made himself the prophet of the Revolution. The *Essay on Privileges*, published in November 1788, denounced the privileges enjoyed by the nobility and the clergy. *What is the Third Estate?*, published in January 1789, called on the people to assert themselves against the two privileged orders that prevailed in state and society alike. The *Views on the Means of which the French People Dispose*, published in February 1789, expounds the principles and methods of reform, and the *Resolutions to Take in the Assemblies*, published in February 1789, gave advice on the procedure to be adopted and the ends to be secured by the local assemblies responsible for electing the members of the States-General.* These four pamphlets, particularly *What is the Third Estate?*, so well expressed the spirit of the time and contained such appropriate ideas on theory and practice that they enjoyed great and immediate success. Sieyès himself became a member of his local constituency assembly and was elected for Paris even though, in accordance with his own principles, the Parisian assembly had resolved that members of the two privileged estates could not be entrusted with the representation of the third estate.

Within the States-General Sieyès immediately came to the fore. In the crucial days of June he led the movement that converted the States-General of three equal and separate orders into the National Assembly in which the orders were integrated. Addressed by Mirabeau as 'master' and described by him as 'Mahomet', Sieyès became a prolific draftsman of decrees and author of pamphlets, but although some of his chief ideas were adopted many were rejected and he enjoyed much less influence than some contemporary and subsequent commentators have believed. As a member of the National Assembly

* The last was an appendix to *Guidance given by His Serene Highness the Duke of Orléans to his representatives in the constituencies*, a text of which Sieyès was not the author.

he was ineligible to the Legislative Assembly of
1791–2 but was elected to the Convention of
1792–5, in which he played an important but in
no way a predominant part. After voting for the
King's death in January 1793, he was somewhat
inactive during the Jacobin ascendency (although
his famous 'I survived' is too modest an account
of his activities during the Terror). In 1795 he
was a member of the Committee of Public
Safety and had a share, though not a great one,
in the preparation of the constitution of 1795. In
the new regime he was a member of the Council
of Five Hundred. After serving as ambassador
to Prussia he became a member of the tottering
Directory in May 1799. Recognising the bank-
ruptcy of the system, he worked for its replacement. Having approached several generals, he
found the right man in Bonaparte and secured
the *coup d'état* of the *18 Brumaire*.

Sieyès had expected to dominate in the new
government but he soon learned his mistake.
Napoleon thought so little of his constitutional
ideas that Sieyès recognised the emptiness of the
suggestion that he should become a consul. Instead he became an ordinary senator. Although
he received honours and awards* he played little
part in affairs. He had some share in plots

* In 1799 he was given the estate of Crosne (for which
other property was soon substituted). Hence the lampoon:

against Napoleon, was absent on the day the
Senate gave Napoleon the title of Emperor, but
refused to testify for General Moreau, charged
with conspiracy. In 1814 he voted for the return
of the Bourbons but in 1815 he joined Napoleon's
Chamber of Peers and publicly supported him
after Waterloo. He was therefore among those
proscribed in 1816. He fled to Brussels, where he
lived until 1830, when he returned to Paris and
survived in failing health until 1836.

Such, in outline, was the career of the man
whom many regarded as *éminence grise* of the
Revolution and as the architect of its constitutions and organic laws. Sieyès was certainly the
instigator of some of the decade's chief events
and the source of some of its chief legislative
ideas. Yet his schemes were rarely adopted in
full, and sometimes they were ignored, denounced, or even wholly rejected. Thus in
August 1789 his draft constitution was not dis-
cussed; in 1790 his ideas on the judicial system
were applied only in part, his schemes for the
clergy, for the government of Paris, and the
censorship of the press were all rejected; in 1792

Sieyès à Bonaparte a fait présent du trône
Sous un pompeux debris croyant l'ensevelir;
Bonaparte à Sieyes à fait présent de Crosne
Pour le payer et l'avilir.
    G. G. van Deusen, *op. cit.*, p. 137.

his reports on the War Department and the education system were adopted by the appropriate committees but denounced by the Jacobins and not adopted by the Convention; in 1793 and 1795 he had little influence on the constitutions adopted in those years; in 1799 he influenced the form rather than the substance of the new constitution.

To some extent these failures were due to himself: his personality frustrated his ability. Cold, sulky and unsympathetic, Sieyès was alone, with collaborators but without friends or disciples. Talking about affairs with what Gouverneur Morris described in 1789 as 'insufferable complacency', appearing to von Humboldt in 1798 as 'too proud and impatient to listen to anything new, much less to accept it', he had a vigorous intellect and a superb vanity. As he told Dumont, 'Politics is a science which I believe I have mastered.'*

As appears even in translation, Sieyès was a master of style, if not of politics. Forceful and uncompromising, his thought was expressed with a clarity and sharpness that greatly increased its impact. The capacity for wit and epigram that he showed in his speech appeared in his writings also.†

* G. G. van Deusen, *op. cit.*, p. 144.

† See, for example, his comments on aristocracy and race (p. 60 below), the privileged orders' attitude to taxation (pp. 96–105), hypocrisy about equality (p. 108), and the English constitution (pp. 106–12).

The message

Mme de Stael told Gouverneur Morris that she thought that the ideas of Sieyès would constitute a new era in politics, just as those of Newton had in physics; this view was shared by Sieyès himself, who was contemptuous of what earlier thinkers had said or written about government.* He did not write any general treatise but from his pamphlets and speeches a doctrine can be extracted: it might be called democratic nationalism. As he declares in *What is the Third Estate?*, 'The nation is prior to everything. It is the source of everything. Its will is always legal; indeed it is the law itself.'† It is with this doctrine that we shall be concerned here; the special message of *What is the Third Estate?* is best studied in the vigorous text of its author. The three main themes of the general doctrine are national unity, popular sovereignty and representative government.

First, the nation and the people are one. As he declared in the summer of 1789 about the terms 'the nation' and 'the people': 'These two terms must be synonymous.'‡ The simple semantic proposition epitomises an impassioned call

* C. A. de Sainte-Beuve, 'L'Abbé Sieyès', *Causeries du Lundi*, 3rd ed., Paris, N. D., vol. V, p. 196.
† See below, p. 124.
‡ G. G. van Deusen, *op. cit.*, p. 76, f.n. 5.

to the ordinary people—the Third Estate—to challenge the privileges and powers of king, nobles and clergy. The unity of the nation must not be violated by the privileges of individuals, classes and localities. Sieyès was an impassioned opponent of all privilege. He regarded the privileges of individuals and classes as irrational in their origin (for even the genuine services of one's ancestors do not make one a more useful or deserving member of society and one's own services are adequately recompensed by ordinary rewards and the esteem of the public), as unjust in their nature (for they are exemptions from the burdens shouldered by other members of the community), and as harmful in their effects (for their beneficiaries usurp positions, rewards and honours undeserved by service or merits, and their victims are cheated, insulted and frustrated). By enjoying a privilege an individual or a class is alienated from the nation.* Before the end of the revolutionary decade he was to carry this doctrine to the ruthless conclusion that other revolutionary leaders have applied to people they hate or fear. He was responsible for the savage sedition law of 1795 and declared in 1799, 'Those who are not of my species are not my fellow men; a noble is not of my species; he is a wolf and I

* *Essay on Privilege, passim; What is the Third Estate?*, p. 58.
B

shoot.'* A similar, but less clearly expressed, exclusion was made at the other end of the social scale. Below the Third Estate composed essentially of people paying direct taxes were a host of people ranging from those who in England would have been called 'the industrious poor' to paupers, vagabonds and brigands—together they might have formed a fifth of the population. By no means all of them were included in the ranks of 'the people' in whom Sieyès wished to vest national sovereignty. It is true that he wanted society to be based on the principle of equality. As he wrote in the summer of 1789:

> The social state must not establish an unjust inequality of rights alongside the natural inequality of means; on the contrary, it protects the equality of rights against the natural but harmful influence of the inequality of means. The social law is not made to weaken the weak and strengthen the strong; on the contrary, it is concerned with putting the weak beyond the range of the strong, and, by covering all citizens with its protective authority, it guarantees to all the full enjoyment of their rights.†

* J. H. Clapham, *op. cit.*, p. 199.
† G. G. van Deusen, *op. cit.*, p. 82, f.n. 27.

Yet he was not a complete egalitarian. He wanted to eliminate legal privileges but not to enfranchise the whole population. He expected that political reform would have beneficial economic and social results for all, but, as will be seen, his proposals for the franchise showed that he did not envisage the immediate establishment of full political equality. There would still be a class that would be, to use Gladstone's expression, 'beyond the pale of the constitution'. The *sans-culottes* were not part of the Third Estate and therefore were not really among his 'people', but his call to 'the people' might well reach them also and thus rally to the cause of the Third Estate those who were outside all the recognised social orders. At times Sieyès seems to talk the language of a universal democracy, but his chief purpose is to advance the cause of a class—the cause of a propertied class.

What has just been said may help to explain the apparent inconsistencies between some of his statements about rights. He firmly believed in the rights which the spokesmen of the Third Estate were asserting, and he drafted a declaration of rights that was among the texts on which the Declaration of 1789 was based. There was one right that was 'more equal than others'. The primacy of the right of property was shown in *The Views*, where in its interest he limited the

sovereignty of the nation by rejecting the idea
that an acceptable solution to the financial problems of the state would be for the state to go
bankrupt. Such an act would violate the sacred
character of private property; neither the King
nor even the nation itself had the right to commit such a crime.*

To deprive any categories of 'the people' of
the rights enjoyed by the rest would be to restore privilege in another form. This applied to
political and non-political rights alike. In *The
Views* he asserted that to deprive a citizen of the
right to be consulted in the adoption of the
laws binding him is to make him a serf and he
told the assembly 'you cannot refuse the quality
of citizen and the rights of citizenship, to this
uninstructed mass, which heavy toil absorbs
completely. Since they must obey the law, just
like you, they must also, just like you, participate in making it. The participation must be
equal.'† Particularly he affirmed that, 'It is not
to *property* but to the *person* that political rights
belong.'‡ Yet he was responsible for a proposal
that contradicted this view: the distinction
between active and passive citizens. The active
citizens, the electorate, should be those adult

* *Ibid.*, p. 29.
† *Ibid.*, p. 82, f.n. 28.
‡ *Ibid.*, p. 82, f.n. 28 also; italics by Sieyès.

males who contributed three livres a year to the public coffers as a voluntary payment. This requirement would exclude from the electorate only the apathetic and the destitute, for even a farm worker could earn almost a livre a day and artisans could earn two or three livres. He suggested that a voluntary contribution of twelve livres should be required of candidates for the assembly. The idea was adopted in a harsher form by the assembly; in the constitution of 1789 a man had to pay three days' wages in ordinary direct taxes to qualify as an active citizen. Sieyès himself looked forward to woman suffrage and favoured giving votes to freed coloureds in the colonies.*

He attacked not only the privileges of the nobility (whom he denounced unreservedly) and of the clergy (whom he considered to be capable of useful public service if they were regulated and paid by the state, which would use the wealth of the Church for educational and charitable purposes), but also the privileges and separatism of localities. Like Burke he insisted that the members of the assembly were not the delegates of their constituents but the representatives of the nation. In July 1789 he induced the assembly to declare that deputies were not bound by the instructions of their constituents—a dec-

* G. G. van Deusen, *op. cit.*, p. 82, f.n. 29, and p. 83, f.n. 31.

laration repeated in many subsequent constitutions and electoral laws. As he said in September: 'The deputy of a bailliwick is directly chosen by his bailliwick, but indirectly he is elected by the sum total of bailliwicks. That is why every deputy is a representative of the whole nation.'* In the summer of 1789 he prepared a scheme for the reorganisation of local government, which he had foreshadowed earlier, which was adopted in its essentials by the assembly, and which is, of course, still largely in force. Of the rational division of the country for administrative purposes he said: 'I know of no better means to make all parts of France into a unit, and all the peoples that divide it into a single nation.'† He was alarmed at the claims of many municipalities in the summer to a freedom of action that meant anarchy, which he abhorred, or federalism, which he rejected. It was necessary for France 'to form a single whole, uniformly submitted in all its parts to the same legislation and a common administration'.‡

National sentiment was to be inculcated also by universal military training every Sunday§ and frequent local and national fêtes devoted to the

* *Ibid.*, p. 77, f.n. 10.
† *Ibid.*, p. 95.
‡ *Ibid.*, p. 85; see also p. 87 for rejection of federalism.
§ *Ibid.*, p. 90.

celebration of morality, civic virtue and the events of the revolution.*

The second main theme of Sieyès's nationalism was that the nation was sovereign. 'All the public authorities, without distinction, are an emanation of the general will; all come from the people, that is to say—from the nation.'† This sovereignty was inalienable. 'No more than an individual can a collection of men renounce the ability to deliberate and to will for its own good.'‡ The nation cannot surrender its powers to anyone nor bind itself to act only in certain ways. As he says in *What is the Third Estate?*, 'It would be ridiculous to suppose that the nation itself could be constricted by the procedures or the constitution to which it has subjected its mandatories. . . . The power exercised by the government . . . is legal only in so far as it is based on the prescribed laws. The national will, on the contrary, never needs anything but its own existence to be legal.'§ One might well say that the referendum of October 1962 was a real exercise of the national will even

* *Ibid.*, pp. 98 ff. Some of his detailed suggestions were taken up by Mirabeau and adopted by the assembly in 1789; others were repeated in his comprehensive report on national education and child welfare, which was rejected by the assembly in 1793.

† *Ibid.*, p. 76.
‡ *Ibid.*, p. 78, f.n. 12.
§ See below, pp. 125–126.

though in holding it the President of the Republic violated the constitutional law binding him. Like Jefferson, Sieyès believed that no constitution could be permanent and that the nation should review its constitution at intervals of thirty years or so, whether or not the need for change was pressing. As with Rousseau, so with Sieyès, the general will was to be identified with the national interest. 'There is no individual, no body, which cannot separate its own private interest from the general interest and thus make itself unjust and criminal. The nation alone is incapable of this for its private interest is the general interest itself.'* Unlike Rousseau, however, Sieyès had no objection to regarding the majority as the spokesmen of the general will. As he declares in *What is the Third Estate?*, 'The law is the expression of the general will, that is to say, the majority.'† He would have no truck with the arid subtleties of Rousseau's distinction between the general will and the will of all or of his criteria for determining whether the general will was being expressed.‡

* G. G. Van Deusen, *op. cit.*, p. 78, f.n. 12.

† See below, p. 80.

‡ Sieyès had little regard for Rousseau: 'A philosopher as perfect in his feelings as he is weak in his views ... his eloquent pages, rich in subsidiary details poor in fundamentals.' C. A. Saint-Beuve, *op. cit.*, p. 194.

The third main theme of Sieyès's nationalism was that the nation expressed itself through representative institutions. He regarded representation as the application to politics of the economists' concept of the division of labour* and compared it favourably with the barbaric methods of direct democracy. The schemes he devised in the earlier years of the Revolution provided for a mass electorate, indirect election, the annual renewal of part of the assembly and the organisation of the unicameral assembly into sections for debating bills but not for voting on them.

The basis of his political systems was a mass electorate, as has already been explained.† The electors were not, however, to be directly responsible for choosing the members of the national legislature. Copying the methods by which the States-General were elected and recommending schemes which were to be adopted in the constitutions and electoral laws of 1791, 1792, 1795 and 1799,‡ he favoured indirect election. Before the States-General met he

* Sieyès prided himself on being the real discoverer of the social art: the general application of this economic principle. *Ibid.*, p. 195.

† See above, p. 14.

‡ See Peter Campbell, *French Electoral Systems and Elections, 1789–1957*, London, 1958, pp. 46–55.

favoured two intermediate stages,* but in several writings on constitutional reform in the summer of 1789 he wanted only one: the active citizens (the electors) of each canton (his subdivision of the Commune, which in its turn was the subdivision of the department) would elect a communal council whose members would be the electorate for the deputies of the National Assembly (and of the members of the departmental council also). Once established, the National Assembly would be renewed by annual partial elections—a third of the deputies vacating their seats each year. The size of each department's representation in the legislative would not depend wholly on the size of its population, despite his view that political rights belonged solely to individuals. A third of the seats in the assembly would be equally divided among the departments, a third would be allocated among them in accordance with their electorates, and a third in accordance with their contributions to the exchequer.

Sieyès believed in a unicameral legislature. He argued, however, that the assembly should be divided into two or three permanent sections which would simultaneously consider a bill in order that the examination should be more

* G. G. van Deusen, *op. cit.*, p. 83, f.n. 32.

thorough; the eventual vote should be by the assembly as a whole.

These three devices—indirect election, annual partial elections and debate by sections—were intended to ensure that representative government did not degenerate into the rash application of policies supported only by a transient majority of the nation. Subject to those provisions, however, the assembly would be untrammelled in its exercise of the legislative power: thus Sieyès vigorously opposed the grant of a veto to the King even although he had no objection to the King possessing the executive power; he shared the view of many reformers that the King could be considered a representative of the nation. Indeed in 1791, after toying with the idea of supporting the Court party, he went so far as to argue against Tom Paine in *Le Moniteur* that liberty might be safer in a monarchy than in a republic; within eighteen months he voted for the King's death.* Yet he never really committed himself in favour of the separation of powers, although he flirted with the concept at the start and end of his constitution-making in *The Views*, when he remarked that the forthcoming assembly should adopt a constitution providing

* The argument was conducted in letters published in *Le Moniteur*.

for the separation of powers, and in his ideas about the constitutions of 1795 and 1799.

His scheme for the reorganisation of the judiciary and the police in March 1790 entailed a partial separation of the judicial power at the lower levels and a complete separation at the national level. Local justices of the peace and lieutenants of police would be directly elected; departmental judges would be chosen by the departmental assembly from the local justices; each departmental assembly would elect from the departmental judges one member of the national judiciary, which would be divided into an appeal court, a political and administrative court, a small court for cases of treason and a small council to supervise the police forces. This scheme had some influence on the system eventually adopted.

As the Revolution progressed, Sieyès became more sceptical of the merits of popular election and representative assembly. In 1795 he criticised the draft constitution and seems to have proposed a silent assembly of nine deputies from each department which would hear bills proposed by the Tribunate of 250 members, representating the people, or by the Government of seven members, representing the state; the Government and the Tribunate would debate a bill before the assembly voted on it. He seems not to have explained how the Tribunate and the Government would be elected. A Constitutional Jury of 100 or 120 members would hear complaints and prepare constitutional amendments for adoption by the assembly and the people. In these ideas can be seen the origins of some of the institutions of 1799. Although it is not certain what his ideas then were, he seems to have wanted a set of mutually balancing powers: a Tribunate to propose laws, a silent Legislative Jury to accept or reject them without debate, a College of Conservators to elect the Tribunate and the Jury, two consuls (one for War and Foreign Affairs, the other for Peace and Domestic Affairs) each choosing a Council of State and ministers to assist him, and a Grand Elector as the ceremonial head of state. These powers would be democratic only very indirectly: six million or so active citizens would choose in their communes one-tenth of their number to be eligible for local posts. The 600,000 members of the communal lists would choose one-tenth of their number to be eligible for departmental posts. The 60,000 members of the departmental lists would choose one-tenth of their number to be eligible for national posts. The College of Conservators could reject one-tenth of the 6,000 members of the national list. The principle was 'confidence from below, authority from above'. This slogan and some of the forms

of Sieyès's plan were all that Napoleon adopted;
incompletely democratic though the former's
scheme was, it was far more democratic than the
one ultimately promulgated.

The legacy

It is not on account of his constitution-mon-
gering that Sieyès deserves to be recalled. His
schemes had only a limited effect on the creators
of the successive regimes of the single decade
between the convocation of the States-General
and the *coup d'état* of *Brumaire*. All the constitutions with which he was concerned were
soon abandoned. The devices which were most
markedly his own have never been adopted by
later constitution-makers. As a constitutionalist
he is of interest only to the historians of his
period.

His lasting importance is as an ideologist of
nationalism, egalitarianism and popular government. His early pamphlets are a passionate call
for popular action against the political and social
privileges which entrenched the power of domi-
nant minorities that had become alien to the
people they exploited. The cause of the Third
Estate in France in 1789 has become a general
cause. Sieyès is in effect the spokesman of
democracy and nationalism everywhere. For he

expressed the fundamental notions of the Revolution that is called French but has really been world-wide. He distilled the spirit of discontent for his own time and a whole subsequent age. *What is the Third Estate?* is a successful recipe for popular revolution.

It challenges comparison with the Communist Manifesto and with Lenin's *What is to be done?* Like the first, it asserted the claims of the many against the few, of the exploited masses against the exploiting minority—although, of course, Marx regarded as exploiters many of the people for whom Sieyès spoke. Unlike the Manifesto, *What is the Third Estate?* contains no general theory about society, the state, their relations and their development. To say this is not to deny that Sieyès had some general principles as the basis of his doctrine. For him the political system was a society of equals based on consent;* its structure and policy followed from that fact, which was, so to speak, the fundamental proposition of his political logic, which applied principles without deference to practice or sentiment. That was his Newtonian revolution in political philosophy. Yet, really, despite his ambitions and his conceit, Sieyès was a propagandist and not a scientist. Like Lenin, he was writing the agenda for a revolutionary movement. But his movement was

* See below, pp. 135–136.

the people as a whole, although, of course, it was individuals and groups that took the lead in the electoral agitation of 1789 and expressed in each constituency the sort of feelings which had caused Sieyès to write. It is noteworthy, and natural, that Sieyès addressed himself to the people at large, in a state where there was freedom for public agitation. Lenin called for professional revolutionaries in a state where repression meant that agitation could be public only at the risk of grave consequences to the individual agitator and the movement to which he belonged. Yet the two men were alike in their ability to see the needs of their cause and, when it arose, the possibilities of a revolutionary situation. It is by this capacity that Sieyès joined the ranks of those philosophers who have succeeded in changing the world.

Our own time has seen the remarkable fusion of the two kinds of revolutionary movement. In Africa and Asia the anti-colonial forces have applied at least the organisational ideas of Lenin in order to promote the egalitarian and nationalist ideas of Sieyès. The conspiratorial party establishing on its triumph a one-party state dedicated to the transformation of society has become familiar through the experience of a score of countries which have developed types of democracy that could well be called 'Jacobin' even if they do not deserve the term 'totalitarian'.* The appeals of such a party echo the language of Sieyès with a vigour that he himself would have approved.

Africans are the Third Estate in a society in which the Europeans are the privileged orders. Their emotions are the same, as Nelson Mandela, the South African nationalist, told the court that was trying him:

> I hate the racial arrogance which decrees that the good things of life shall be retained as the exclusive right of a minority of the population, and which reduces the majority of the population to a subservience and inferiority, and maintains them as voteless chattels to work where they are told and behave as they are told by the ruling minority.

Like the members of the Third Estate, the Africans may enter honourable professions but be debarred from reaching the top. Again in the words of Mandela:

> In the Courts where we practised we were constantly aware that no matter how well, how correctly, how adequately we pursued

* See the vigorous analysis in J. L. Talmon, *The Origins of Totalitarian Democracy*, London, 1952.

C

our career of law, we could not become a prosecutor or a magistrate or a judge. We became aware of the fact that as attorneys we often dealt with officials whose competence and attainments were no higher than ours, but whose superior position was maintained and protected by a white skin.†

The French aristocrats claimed to be of superior birth because they were the descendants of the conquering German invaders. As Sieyès dealt with that claim so do African nationalists deal with the similar claims of the Europeans.

Nationalism demands that the interests of indigenous peoples should dominate over those of aliens because the country belongs to the indigenous peoples. Socialism demands that the interests of the workers should dominate over those of their employers because their contribution to the creation of wealth is more significant than that of their bosses. Democracy demands that those of the majority should dominate over those of the minority because they are a majority. In Africa in general and in South Africa in particular the African people are

† *The Observer*, London, November 18, 1962, p. 11. Compare below, p. 54–56.

indigenous to the soil, are the real workers, and are the majority. Their right to the effective control of their own interests is therefore unchallengeable.*

Just as the French aristocrat could work his passage and reintegrate himself into the nation by abandoning his privileges so can the European. In the words of the first manifesto of the Front de Libération Nationale in Algeria:

> All French citizens desiring to remain in Algeria will be allowed to opt for their original nationality, in which case they will be considered as foreigners, or for Algerian nationality, in which case they will be considered as Algerians, both as to rights and duties.†

The same applies to native aristocrats, as indicated in this quotation from an election issue of the newspaper of the Guinea Democratic Party.

> Diallo Saifoulaye, like La Fayette on the night of August 4, 1789, has renounced his

* P. N. Raboroko, a leader of the Pan-Africanist Congress in South Africa, quoted in P. van Rensburg, *Guilty Land*, London, 1962, p. 150. See below, pp. 59–60.

† Quoted in E. Behr, *The Algerian Problem*, London, 1961, p. 169. See below, p. 173.

privileges in order to join the democratic camp, with a view to relieving the people's misery, supporting them in their struggles for the conquest of their rights.*

But, of course, the destruction of a regime based on inequality and oligarchy is intended to be only the prelude to the establishment of a new one based on equality and democracy. As in eighteenth-century France, so in twentieth-century Africa, the success of democracy and progress requires the elimination of the ancient divisions among the people. In the words of Sékou Touré:

> To sum up, we can say that our state is democratic, unitary, and progressive. Its object is to make Guinea a viable national entity. In three or four years no one should remember the tribal, ethnic, and religious rivalries which, in the recent past, have done so much harm to our country and its people.†

To cite these parallels is, of course, only to say again that the French Revolution is of lasting

* Quoted in T. Hodgkin, *African Political Parties*, London, 1961, p. 156.
† *Ibid.*, p. 157.

significance because the essential features of the situation in which it occurred are likely to appear in other societies. If a political prisoner in South Africa or a ruling party in West Africa uses language that might have come from Sieyès it is not because of the direct influence of his personal message (even in the French-speaking countries) but because of the recurrence of the situation in which he acted. Yet, even so, in tracing the general legacy of the Revolution we should not forget that Sieyès himself was among the revolutionaries who set no racial bounds to the application of their principles. In advocating the grant of political rights to the coloured peoples in the colonies France then had, they showed that their principles were for export everywhere—even where their adoption might weaken the power of France herself. In this way Sieyès and those who thought like him on this issue showed themselves prophetically aware of the true universality of the French Revolution.

Chronological Note
The Pre-Revolution, 1786–8
by S. E. Finer

Sieyès's *What is the Third Estate?* was written in November and December 1788. After more than a year of pressures, public agitation and popular disturbances, the French government had finally consented to convene the States-General in 1789. But this archaic body had not met since 1614. The great question, therefore, was whether it should meet according to the ancient mode of 1614, i.e. as three separate orders—the orders of the Clergy, of the Nobility and of the Third Estate. The leaders of the middle classes were demanding and indeed expecting that the Third Estate would have as many representatives as the first two orders combined; and most of them also demanded that voting in the States-General should be by heads, not by orders.

On September 25, 1788, however, their hopes were sharply rebuffed. The most important and

influential of the public bodies to demand the
recall of the States-General had been the great
Parlement of Paris. This now pronounced that the
States-General must meet according to the ancient
forms of 1614. At once a clamour of protest arose
from individuals, corporations and municipalities
from one end of the kingdom to the other, all
remonstrating against the pronouncement and
advancing the claims of the Third Estate. Of all
such expressions of opinion, Sieyès's pamphlet
was, by contemporary accounts, the most influential.

In one sense its arguments are timeless:
Sieyès insisted on bringing the argument back to
first principles, and these can therefore be adjudged for what they are worth irrespective of the
time and the circumstances which led him to
express them. Yet, necessarily, he makes references to the events and controversies of the
day.

Unexplained, these references might puzzle and
indeed provoke the reader who is unfamiliar with
the period. Accordingly, I have supplied brief
explanatory notes. But even these would prove
confusing without an outline of the main sequence
of events in the order in which they occurred.
Hence the need for a chronological summary at
the very outset. Here no more is attempted than
the bare sequence of events; more detailed

explanations will be found in the individual notes to the text.

The events of 1786–8, the *Pre-Révolution Française*, fall into three periods, viz. (1) The opposition of the First Assembly of the Notables to the fiscal and administrative reforms of Calonne (February 22–May 25, 1787), (2) The opposition of the *Parlements* to the fiscal measures of Brienne and the judicial reforms of Lamoignon (July 1787–August 25, 1788) and (3) Third Estate versus the Privileged Orders (September 25–December 27, 1788).

I. The First Assembly of Notables and the measures of Calonne.

Since 1783, which marked the close of France's successful warfare as ally of the American colonies against Britain, the French Controller General of Finance had been Calonne. The war had left the French monarchy loaded with debt. Faced with a vast deficit, by 1786 Calonne recognised that he could no longer make do by further borrowing and that nothing short of a radical reform of the French taxation system would suffice. On August 20, 1786, he presented a memorandum to King Louis XVI. Of the reforms proposed in this document two were outstanding. First, Calonne proposed to substitute a new tax for the *vingtièmes*.

The *vingtièmes* were direct taxes of 5% of the income derived from land, house property, public offices and industry. In 1786 there were three *vingtièmes* in existence; the first, imposed in 1749, ran for a fixed term; the second, imposed in 1760, was due to lapse in 1790; and the third, imposed in 1782, was due to lapse at the end of 1786. For the first and second *vingtièmes* levied on *land*, Calonne proposed to levy a new tax; this was to be a proportional land tax (*subvention territoriale*), to be borne by all proprietors without distinction, graduated according to the productiveness of the soil, and levied in kind.

Furthermore, to ensure the just and universal distribution of this new tax, Calonne proposed that the assessment be put in the hands of the taxpayers themselves, by entrusting the allocation of the tax to new and elective bodies, the Provincial Assemblies. In some parts of France, known as the *Pays d'Etats*, the ancient Provincial Estates still functioned; the new assemblies were not to be established in these areas, but in those others, known as the *Pays d'Elections*, which had no representative assemblies and were governed directly by the Crown. These Provincial Assemblies would be elected by the local proprietors and would undertake, under supervision by the Royal Intendant, the allocation of the new tax (Note 7, p. 202).

Athwart the path of such reforms lay the certain opposition of the thirteen *Parlements*, or sovereign courts; and pre-eminently that of the *Parlement* of Paris. To be legally valid, all royal edicts and laws had to be registered in these courts; but in the course of centuries they had acquired the right to remonstrate that the laws presented to them for registration were inconsistent with previous legislation or incompatible with the fundamental laws of the French kingdom, and sometimes they even refused to register them at all. In such a case the King was wont to hold a royal session of the *Parlement*, called a *lit de justice;* here, in person, he could command registration. The royal lawyers maintained that this procedure was a valid registration. The *Parlements* held that it was not. On occasion they refused to recognize the validity of the *lit de justice*. Thereupon the King could only prevail by *force majeure*: he would exile the members of the court to some out of the way place until they changed their minds. In the course of the eighteenth century the *Parlements* had fought a running battle with the monarchy over a whole range of issues. As Montesquieu argued in his *Esprit de Lois*, the *Parlements* had thereby tempered the royal despotism; but as they consisted of a closed self-perpetuating oligarchy of individuals whose functions automatically entitled them to nobility and the fiscal immunities which this conferred, they tempered despotism only at the price of obstructing much-needed administrative, social and above all fiscal reforms (Note 20, p. 207).

Calonne was certain that the *Parlements* would refuse to sanction his proposals. Accordingly he decided to by-pass them by getting his plans underwritten by a consultative assembly of great names drawn from the great corporations and institutions of the kingdom, e.g. the Princes of the Blood, the Church, the nobility, the municipalities. Hence, December 29, the convocation of the Notables. They met February 22, 1787, and Calonne put his proposals before them.

His tactics completely misfired, for the Notables proved quite intransigent. They radically opposed his proposed land tax and would agree to the Provincial Assemblies only with important modifications. Calonne's plans for these bodies failed to provide, in respect of either their election, composition or procedure, for the distinction between the three orders. The Notables demanded such a distinction and they were particularly incensed by the possibility of the new bodies being presided over by a member of the Third Estate instead of a member of one or other of the two privileged orders.

On April 8, Calonne was dismissed, and was succeeded, on May 1, 1787, by one of his foremost opponents amongst the Notables, Lomenie de Brienne, the Archbishop of Toulouse. Brienne thought he could manipulate the Notables. He agreed with them that the Provincial Assemblies should be constituted by orders and that the presidency should alternate between the two privileged orders. He asked, however, that the representatives of the Third Estate should constitute two-thirds of the total membership. The Notables refused to agree and proposed instead that Third Estate representation should only be equal to that of the other two orders combined. To this Brienne agreed. Since many of the representatives of the Third Estate would be noblemen, this 50–50 basis ensured the preponderance of the privileged orders in the new assemblies.

When Brienne put new proposals for the land tax before the Notables, however, he met with blank refusal. The Notables excused themselves by the argument that they had no authority to sanction any such fiscal arrangements and that this could only be done lawfully through the *Parlements*; indeed, they said, possibly by only the States-General. On May 25, therefore, Brienne dismissed the Notables. His only course now was to confront the *Parlements*—the very step that the Notables had been summoned to avoid.

II. The opposition of the Parlements *to the fiscal measures of Brienne and the judicial reforms of Lamoignon (July 1787–August 25, 1788).*

The *Parlement* of Paris acted just as Calonne had predicted. It did indeed register a few of Brienne's minor fiscal measures and it even registered the law for the Provincial Assemblies; but on July 30 it rejected his land tax. On the pretext that this was a tax of indefinite duration, it pronounced itself incompetent to register it and stated that only the States-General could legally do so. This action proved vastly popular throughout France. The *Parlement*, it appeared, was resisting depotism and demanding the recall of a representative assembly. Henceforth throughout its struggle with the Crown the *Parlement* was to retain this public support and to appear as the bastion of popular liberties against autocratic tyranny.

On August 6, the King held a solemn *lit de justice* and pronounced the registration of the land tax. The *Parlement* responded by declaring the *lit de justice* unconstitutional. The King therefore, on August 14, exiled the *Parlement* to Troyes. Everywhere its stand was supported—by the provincial *Parlements* and by public opinion generally. In some places this popular support was marked by demonstrations and rioting.

Meanwhile Brienne sought a compromise. On September 19 he agreed to withdraw the proposed land tax provided that the *Parlement* would sanction the extension of the second *vingtième* (due to expire in 1790) to the year 1792. In return he promised to convene the States-General in 1792. Brienne had no real faith in the States-General, but had calculated that by 1792 he would have restored order to the finances and that the convocation of the States-General would therefore prove unnecessary. Another part of the bargain he struck with the *Parlement* was that this body would raise no obstruction to further public loans. Amid scenes of wild rejoicing, the *Parlement* returned to Paris. On November 18, the King warned it that he would, next day, be presenting his proposals for a public loan in a special royal session. Such a session resembled a *lit de justice* except that the magistrates were permitted to express their views on the proposed legislation. So, at the royal session on November 19, the *Parlement* debated the proposals for the loan; but at its close the King formally pronounced the edict as registered. At this the magistrates remonstrated violently; and among them the Duke of Orléans rose to declare that the action of the King was actually illegal. For this temerity he was instantly exiled, while two of the leading magistrates were sent to prison.

From the beginning of the new year, 1788, the

Parlement undertook a systematic harassment of the King and his ministers. In January it censured *lettres de cachet*. In April it renewed its remonstrances against the allegedly illegal registration of the public loan. Then, sensing that some royal action was being prepared against it, it issued, on May 3, 1788, a declaration of what it understood to be the fundamental laws of the kingdom of France. Significantly this included the proposition that new taxes could be levied only with the consent of the States-General. The next day royal troops arrested its two ringleaders and on May 8 the government carried out a *coup d'état*. In the presence of his troops the King, in a solemn *lit de justice*, registered six edicts. The effect of these was not simply to reform the whole system of the courts of first-instance in France; in addition the age-old right of the *Parlements* to register laws and edicts common to the whole realm was withdrawn from them. In their place, registration would be effected by a new court (or rather the revival of a very ancient one) the so-called *Cour Plénière*. Nominated by the Crown this was confidently expected to be more pliant to the royal wishes than the *Parlements* (Note 20, p. 207).

This action provoked widespread rioting throughout the country. Grounds for public disorder had been steadily maturing. For one thing, when the new Provincial Assemblies came to be set up, they were not elected: instead, the Crown nominated half their members who then proceeded to co-opt to make up their full number. In most cases the Third Estate was forced to be represented by nobles and clerics. Again, in some provinces the local *Parlements* were jealous of the new assemblies and tried to wreck them—as in Bordeaux and Toulouse. In Béarn and Brittany and Dauphiné the *Parlements* incited mobs to riot by appealing to the strong separatist sentiments of these localities. In other *Pays d'Etats*, e.g. in Hainault, Provence as well as in Dauphiné, local movements arose seeking to revive their Provincial Estates. In May there were riots in Pau and Rennes; in June, in Dauphiné. It was reported that the temper of the troops was becoming uncertain.

Meanwhile Brienne had become desperate for ready cash. He got the first order, i.e. the clergy, to convene an extraordinary session of their assembly and asked it for a large '*don gratuit*'. The assembly met in May 1788 only to condemn his judicial reforms and to demand, like the *Parlements* and the public, the recall of the States-General. The sum of money voted was derisory. Brienne began to bend. On July 5, he suspended the decree creating the *Cour Plénière* and announced that the States-General was to be summoned. The public was asked to submit information and views on the way in which it had been or

D

ought to be constituted and for this purpose the censorship was lifted. The result was a vast effervescence of public opinion and a veritable hail of pamphlets. On August 8, Brienne yielded still further: he now announced that the States-General would be convened in a few months—namely on May 1, 1789. For the Treasury was empty. On August 16, Brienne suspended Treasury payments till September and began to repay debt in paper money. Through the Queen and the Court he tried to secure the assistance of Necker, the former Director-General of Finance, very skilful at handling loans. But Necker refused to serve under Brienne. On August 25, Brienne resigned and Necker was named Director-General of Finance in his place.

III. *Third Estate versus Privileged Orders* (*August 25, 1788–December 27, 1788*).

Unlike Brienne, who never really wanted to convene the States-General, Necker expected great things from such an assembly. Hence, apart from short-term measures to restore financial credit, he confined himself to bringing about the recall of the States-General and to ensuring that in it the Third Estate should have a representation equal to that of the other two orders combined. He even hoped that on financial issues, though not on others, voting would go by heads and not by orders.

An arrangement of this sort was being widely canvassed as a result of the disorders in Dauphiné. There, in July, nobles and commoners had alike demanded from Brienne the right to revive their Provincial Estates. When Brienne refused they met illegally at Vizille and there agreed that in their Estates the representation of the Third Estate should be equal to that of the two other orders combined, and that voting should be by head and not by order. After this Brienne yielded and conceded them the right to reconstitute their Estates, and in September 1788, just after Necker took office, their representatives were meeting as a constituent assembly to draft a constitution for this body (Note 2, p. 200).

Necker's first act was to reconvene the *Parlement* of Paris, the spearhead of popular resistance to royal despotism—as it then seemed. It returned to Paris on September 23 amid delirious rejoicing, only, on September 25, to cast away its popularity and prestige for ever. On that day it pronounced that the forthcoming States-General must meet as in 1614; i.e. that it must vote by orders and not by heads and that there must be no 'doubling' of the Third Estate's representation.

From this moment the political struggle changed character. Hitherto it had been an aristocratic *fronde* against the monarchy. Now it became a struggle of the Third Estate against the other two orders. There formed what became known as the patriotic or national 'party', though it was not a party in the current sense of the word but a personal connexion of individuals and cliques meeting in coffee houses, clubs and freemasons' lodges. There was in addition a mysterious 'Committee of Thirty' (including Sieyès among its numbers) whose role is still largely unknown but which corresponded and kept contact with individuals and societies throughout France. This 'party' tried to bring pressure on the government by a vigorous pamphlet warfare and by a campaign to get the municipal authorities throughout France to petition the government with demands for the 'doubling' of the Third Estate's representation and for voting by heads instead of voting by orders (Note 2, p. 200 and Note 26, p. 212).

Dismayed by the declaration of the Paris *Parlement* Necker fell into the same trap as his two predecessors, Calonne and Brienne. He thought that he could presume upon getting a favourable response from the Notables and then utilise this to offset the pronouncement of the *Parlement* of Paris. He therefore reconvened the Notables but this time for one purpose alone: to advise on the 'most regular and appropriate way of constituting the States-General' (Note 12, p. 205). The Notables re-convened on November 6, 1788. To Necker's disgust they rejected by an overwhelming majority the proposal to make the Third Estate's representation equal to that of the other two orders combined. As to voting by head and not by order, this was not even put to a vote at all. Thus the privileged Notables re-echoed the privileged *Parlement* (Note 9, p. 204, and Note 23, p. 210), but interposed, as a sort of consolation to the Third Estate, a solemn avowal of their wish to see complete fiscal equality between the three orders. Necker prorogued the Notables on December 12, 1788; but even as he was doing so five Princes of the Blood (who sat in the assembly) published their *Mémoire au Roi*. Provoked beyond endurance by the attacks of the 'national party', they revindicated their privileges and contemptuously advised the Third Estate to confine its attention to reducing taxation—promising that if it behaved itself in this manner, they would in return consent to fiscal equality (Note 24, p. 210).

Necker now carried the fight to the royal Council and there, after prolonged discussions, induced the King to come some part of the way towards him. The document, the *Résultat du Conseil* of December 27, 1788, declared that in the forthcoming States-General the representation of the Third Estate was to be equal to that of the other two orders combined. However, nothing was said as to whether the voting would be by head or by order. The privileged orders maintained that it implicitly rejected this step, but the Third Estate maintained that on the contrary it implicitly entailed this. So both sides claimed victory and the public controversy continued as acrimoniously as before (Note 31, p. 212). (In his unpublished report to the Council, however, Necker had made it clear that voting by order would continue to be legally binding on the States-General unless the procedure was altered by common agreement of all three orders with the King's consent. But nobody knew this.)

The *Résultat du Conseil* is the latest incident mentioned in Sieyès's pamphlet. It is at this point therefore that this historical summary can conveniently end.

What is the
Third Estate?

What is the Third Estate? [a]

'*As long as the Philosopher does not go beyond the boundary of truth, do not accuse him of going too far. His function is to show us the goal and first, therefore, he must get there. If he stopped and dared to put up his signpost midway, it might misdirect us. The duty of the Administrator is the reverse. He has to set his pace according to the nature of the difficulties. . . . If the Philosopher has not reached the goal, he does not know where he stands. If the Administrator does not see the goal, he does not know where he goes.*'

The plan of this book is fairly simple. We must ask ourselves three questions.

1) What is the Third Estate? *Everything.*

2) What has it been until now in the political order? *Nothing.*

3) What does it want to be? *Something*.

We are going to see whether the answers are correct. Meanwhile, it would be improper to say these statements are exaggerated until the supporting evidence has been examined.* We shall next examine the measures that have been tried and those that must still be taken for the Third Estate really to become something. Thus, we shall state:

4) What the Ministers have attempted and what even the privileged orders propose to do for it.

5) What ought to have been done.

6) Finally, what remains to be done in order that the Third Estate should take its rightful place.

* This sentence did not appear in the First Edition.

CHAPTER I

The Third Estate is a Complete Nation

What does a nation require to survive and prosper? It needs *private* activities and *public* services.

These private activities can all be comprised within four classes of persons:

1) Since land and water provide the basic materials for human needs, the first class, in logical order, includes all the families connected with work on the land.

2) Between the initial sale of goods and the moment when they reach the consumer or user, goods acquire an increased value of a more or less compound nature through the incorporation of varying amounts of labour. In this way human industry manages to improve the gifts of nature and the value of the raw material may be multiplied twice, or ten-fold, or a hundred-fold. Such are the activities of the second class of persons.

3) Between production and consumption, as also between the various stages of production, a variety of intermediary agents intervene, to help producers as well as consumers; these are the dealers and the merchants. Merchants continually compare needs according to place and time and estimate the profits to be obtained from warehousing and transportation; dealers undertake, in the final stage, to deliver the goods on the wholesale and retail markets. Such is the function of the third class of persons.

4) Besides these three classes of useful and industrious citizens who deal with *things* fit to be consumed or used, society also requires a vast number of special activities and of services *directly* useful or pleasant to the *person*. This fourth class embraces all sorts of occupations, from the most distinguished liberal and scientific professions to the lowest of menial tasks.

Such are the activities which support society. But who performs them? The Third Estate.

Public services can also, at present, be divided into four known categories, the army, the law, the Church and the bureaucracy. It needs no detailed analysis to show that the Third Estate everywhere constitutes nineteen-twentieths of them, except that it is loaded with all the really arduous work, all the tasks which the privileged order refuses to perform. Only the well-paid and honorific posts are filled by members of the privileged order. Are

we to give them credit for this? We could do so
only if the Third Estate was unable or unwilling
to fill these posts. We know the answer. Nevertheless, the privileged have dared to preclude the
Third Estate. 'No matter how useful you are', they
said, 'no matter how able you are, you can go so far
and no further. Honours are not for the like of you.'
The rare exceptions, noticeable as they are bound
to be, are mere mockery, and the sort of language
allowed on such occasions is an additional insult.

If this exclusion is a social crime, a veritable act of
war against the Third Estate, can it be said at least
to be useful to the commonwealth? Ah! Do we not
understand the consequences of monopoly? While
discouraging those it excludes, does it not destroy
the skill of those it favours? Are we unaware that
any work from which free competition is excluded
will be performed less well and more expensively?

When any function is made the prerogative of
a separate order among the citizens, has nobody
remarked how a salary has to be paid not only to
the man who actually does the work, but to all
those of the same caste who do not, and also to
the entire families of both the workers and the
non-workers? Has nobody observed that as soon
as the government becomes the property of a
separate class, it starts to grow out of all proportion and that posts are created not to meet the
needs of the governed but of those who govern

them? Has nobody noticed that while on the one hand, we basely and I dare say *stupidly* accept this situation of ours, on the other hand, when we read the history of Egypt or stories of travels in India, we describe the same kind of conditions as despicable, monstrous, destructive of all industry, as inimical to social progress, and above all as debasing to the human race in general and intolerable to Europeans in particular . . . ?[b] But here we must leave considerations which, however much they might broaden and clarify the problem, would nevertheless slow our pace.[c]

It suffices to have made the point that the so-called usefulness of a privileged order to the public service is a fallacy; that, without help from this order, all the arduous tasks in the service are performed by the Third Estate; that without this order the higher posts could be infinitely better filled; that they ought to be the natural prize and reward of recognised ability and service; and that if the privileged have succeeded in usurping all well-paid and honorific posts, this is both a hateful iniquity towards the generality of citizens and an act of treason to the commonwealth.

Who is bold enough to maintain that the Third Estate does not contain within itself everything needful to constitute a complete nation? It is like a strong and robust man with one arm still in chains. If the privileged order were removed, the nation would not be something less but something more. What then is the Third Estate? All; but an 'all' that is fettered and oppressed. What would it be without the privileged order? It would be all; but free and flourishing. Nothing will go well without the Third Estate; everything would go considerably better without the two others.

It is not enough to have shown that the privileged, far from being useful to the nation, can only weaken and injure it; we must prove further that the nobility*d* is not part of our society at all: it may be a *burden* for the nation, but it cannot be part of it.

First, it is impossible to find what place to assign to the caste of nobles among all the elements of a nation.*e* I know that there are many people, all too many, who, from infirmity, incapacity, incurable idleness or a collapse of morality, perform no functions at all in society. Exceptions and abuses always exist alongside the rule, and particularly in a large commonwealth. But all will agree that the fewer these abuses, the better organised a state is supposed to be. The most ill-organised state of all would be the one where not just isolated individuals but a complete class of citizens would glory in inactivity amidst the general movement and contrive to consume the best part of the product without having in any way helped to produce it. Such a class, surely, is foreign to the nation because of its *idleness*.

The nobility, however, is also a foreigner in our midst because of its *civil and political* prerogatives. (What is a nation? A body of associates living under *common* laws and represented by the same *legislative assembly*, etc.)

Is it not obvious that the nobility possesses privileges and exemptions which it brazenly calls its rights and which stand distinct from the rights of the great body of citizens? Because of these special rights, the nobility does not belong to the common order, nor is it subjected to the common laws. Thus its private rights make it a people apart in the great nation. It is truly *imperium in imperio*.

As for its *political* rights, it also exercises these separately from the nation. It has its own representatives who are charged with no mandate from the People. Its deputies sit separately, and even if they sat in the same chamber as the deputies of ordinary citizens they would still constitute a different and separate representation. They are foreign to the nation first because of their origin, since they do not owe their powers to the People; and secondly because of their aim, since this consists in defending, not the general interest, but the private one.

The Third Estate then contains everything that pertains to the nation while nobody outside the Third Estate can be considered as part of the nation. What is the Third Estate? *Everything.*[f]

CHAPTER 2

What has the Third Estate been until now? Nothing

We shall examine neither the condition of servitude in which the People has suffered for so long, nor that of constraint and humiliation in which it is still confined. Its status has changed in private law. It must change still further: the nation as a whole cannot be free, nor can any of its separate orders, unless the Third Estate is free. Freedom does not derive from privileges. It derives from the rights of citizens—and these rights belong to all.

If the aristocrats try to repress the People at the expense of that very freedom of which they prove themselves unworthy, the Third Estate will dare challenge their right. If they reply, 'by the right of conquest', one must concede that this is to go back rather far. Yet the Third Estate need not fear examining the past. It will betake itself to the year preceding the 'conquest'; and as it is nowadays too strong to be conquered it will certainly

E   59

resist effectively. Why should it not repatriate to the Franconian forests all the families who wildly claim to descend from the race of the conquerors and to inherit their *rights of conquest*?

If it were purged in this way, I think the nation might well recover from the thought that thenceforward it would be reduced to the descendants of mere Gauls and Romans. When our poor fellow-citizens insist on distinguishing between one lineage and another, could nobody reveal to them that it is at least as good to be descended from the Gauls and the Romans as from the Sicambrians, Welches and other savages from the woods and swamps of ancient Germany? 'True enough,' some will say; 'but conquest has upset all relationships and hereditary nobility now descends through the line of the conquerors.' Well, then; we shall have to arrange for it to descend through the other line! The Third Estate will become noble again by becoming a conqueror in its own turn.[1]

But, if we accept that all races are mixed; if the blood of the Franks (none the better for being pure) now mingles with the blood of the Gauls; if the fathers of the Third Estate are the fathers of the whole nation; can we not hope that one day will see the end of this long parricide which one class is proud to commit day after day against all the others? Why should not reason and justice, eventually grown as powerful as vanity, press so hard upon the privileged order that, moved by a new, truer and more social interest, it requests its own *regeneration* within the order of the Third Estate?*

Let us pursue our theme. By Third Estate is meant all the citizens who belong to the common order. Anybody who holds a legal privilege of any kind deserts the common order, stands as an exception to the common laws and, consequently, does not belong to the Third Estate. As we have already said, a nation is made one by virtue of common laws and common representation. It is indisputably only too true that in France a man who is protected only by the common laws is a nobody; whoever is totally unprivileged must submit to every form of contempt, insult and humiliation. To avoid being completely crushed, what must the unlucky non-privileged person do? He has to attach himself by all kinds of contemptible actions to some magnate; he prostitutes his principles and human dignity for the possibility of claiming, in his need, the protection of a *somebody*.

But we are less concerned in this book with the civil rights of the Third Estate than with its

* In the First Edition this paragraph ran thus: 'If we see in the privileged order, which is the constant enemy of the Third Estate, that which is alone in fact observable there, viz. the children of this same Third Estate, how are we to describe the parricidal audacity with which the privileged hate, despise and oppress their brothers?'

relationship to the constitution. Let us see what part it plays in the States-General.

Who have been its so-called 'Representatives'? Men who have been raised to the nobility or have received temporary privileges. These bogus deputies have not even been always freely elected by the People. In the States-General sometimes, and in the Provincial Estates almost always, the representation of the People is considered as inherent in the holder of certain offices.

The old aristocracy detests new nobles; it allows nobles to sit as such only when they can prove, as the phrase goes, 'four generations and a hundred years'. Thus it relegates the other nobles to the order of the Third Estate to which, obviously, they no longer belong.[g]

In law, however, all nobles are equal—those whose nobility dates from yesterday just as much as those who succeed for better or for worse in hiding their origins or their usurpation. In law all have the same privileges. Only *opinion* distinguishes between them. But if the Third Estate must endure a prejudice sanctioned by law, there is no reason why it should submit to a prejudice contrary to law.

Let them create as many noblemen as they like; it still remains certain that the moment any citizen is granted privileges against the common laws, he no longer forms part of the common order. His new interest is contrary to the general interest; he becomes incompetent to vote in the name of the People.

According to the same undeniable principle, those who merely hold temporary privileges must also be debarred from representing the Third Estate. Their interest, too, is in greater or lesser part opposed to the common interest; and although opinion assigns them to the Third Estate and the law does not mention them, the nature of things, stronger than both opinion and the law, sets them irresistibly apart from the common order.

It is objected that to remove from the Third Estate not only those with hereditary privileges, but even those with mere temporary ones, is to try, from sheer wantonness, to weaken that order by depriving it of its more enlightened, courageous and esteemed members.

The last thing I want to do is to diminish the strength or dignity of the Third Estate, since, in my mind, it is completely coincident with my idea of a nation. But can we, whatever our motives, arrange for truth to cease to be truth? If an army has the misfortune to be deserted by its best soldiers, are these the troops it entrusts with the defence of its camp? One cannot say it too often: any privilege runs contrary to common laws; hence, all those who enjoy privileges, without exception, constitute a separate class opposed to the Third Estate. At the same time, I must point out that this should not alarm the friends of the People. On the contrary, it takes us back to the higher national interest by showing the urgent necessity for immediately suppressing all temporary privileges[h] which split the Third Estate and may seem to oblige it to put its destiny in its enemies' hands. Besides, this remark must not be separated from the ensuing one: the abolition of privileges within the Third Estate does not mean the loss of immunities which some of its members enjoy. Such immunities are nothing but common rights and it was totally unjust to deprive the main part of the People of them. Thus, I am not calling for the loss of a right but for its restitution;[i] and should it be objected that the universalisation of certain privileges—e.g. not balloting for militia service[j]—would make it impossible to satisfy various public needs, my answer is that any public need is the responsibility of everybody and not of a separate class of citizens, and that one must be as ill-acquainted with reasoning as with fairness if one cannot think of a more national means of constituting and maintaining whatever kind of army one wants to have.

Consequently, either because they were never elected at all; or because they were not elected by the full membership of the Third Estate of towns and rural areas who were entitled to representation; or because, owing to their privileges, they were not even eligible; the so-called deputies of the Third Estate who have sat until now in the States-General never had a real mandate from the People.*

Some occasionally express surprise at hearing complaints about a three-fold 'aristocracy composed of the army, the Church and the law'. They insist that this is only a figure of speech; yet the phrase must be understood strictly. If the States-General is the interpreter of the general will, and correspondingly has the right to make laws, it is this capacity, without doubt, that makes it a true aristocracy: whereas the States-General as we know it at present is simply a *clerico-nobili-judicial* assembly.

Add to this appalling truth the fact that, in one way or another, all departments of the executive have also fallen into the hands of the caste that provides the Church, the law and the army. As a result of a spirit of brotherhood or *comradeship*, nobles always prefer each other to the rest of the nation. The usurpation is total; in every sense of the word, they reign.

If you consult history in order to verify whether the facts agree or disagree with my description, you will discover, as I did, that it is a great mistake to believe that France is a monarchy. With the exception of a few years under Louis XI and

* This paragraph did not appear in the First Edition.

under Richelieu and a few moments under Louis XIV when it was plain despotism, you will believe you are reading the history of a *Palace* aristocracy. It is not the King who reigns; it is the Court. The Court has made and the Court has unmade; the Court has appointed ministers and the Court has dismissed them; the Court has created posts and the Court has filled them. . . . And what is the Court but the head of this vast aristocracy which overruns every part of France, which seizes on everything through its members, which exercises everywhere every essential function in the whole administration? So that in its complaints the People has grown used to distinguishing between the monarch and those who exercise power. It has always considered the King as so certainly misled and so defenceless in the midst of the active and all-powerful Court, that it has never thought of blaming him for all the wrongs done in his name.

Finally, is it not enough simply to open our eyes to what is occurring around us at this very moment? What do we see? The aristocracy on its own, fighting simultaneously against reason, justice, the People, the minister and the King. The end of this terrible battle is still undecided. Can it still be said that the aristocracy is only a chimera!

Let us sum up: to this very day, the Third Estate has never had genuine representatives in the States-General. Thus its political rights are null.

CHAPTER 3

What does the Third Estate want to be? Something

It is wrong to judge the claims of the Third Estate from the isolated remarks of certain authors who are partially aware of the rights of man. The Third Estate is still very backward in this matter, not only by comparison with the insight of students of the social order, but also with that mass of common ideas which constitutes public opinion. The authentic requests of the Third Estate can only be adjudged through the formal demands which the great municipalities of the kingdom have addressed to the government.[2] What do we see therein? That the People wants to become *something*, and in fact, the least thing possible. It wants to have 1) genuine representatives in the States-General, i.e. deputies *drawn from its own ranks* and competent to interpret its wishes and defend its interests. But what good would it do the Third Estate to participate in the States-General if the interest opposed to its own were to preponderate there? It would simply sanction by its presence the oppression of which it would be the everlasting victim. Therefore, it most certainly cannot come and vote in the States-General unless its influence there *is at least equal to that of the privileged orders*. So it asks for 2) a number of representatives equal to that of the other two orders taken together. However, this equality of representation would become entirely illusory if each chamber voted separately. The Third Estate, therefore, asks for 3) the votes to be counted *by heads and not by orders*.[k] Such is the whole extent of the claims which appear to have so alarmed the privileged orders; and for this reason alone have these come round to believing that the reform of abuses has become indispensable.

The Third Estate's modest aim is to possess an equal influence in the States-General to that of the privileged orders. Once again, could it ask for less? And is it not clear that if its influence is less than equal, it cannot hope to come out of its political non-existence and become *something*?

However, the great pity of it all is that the three articles which constitute the claim of the Third Estate are not enough to give it the equal influence which it cannot effectively dispense with. To grant it no more than an equal number of representatives drawn from its own ranks will be useless: for the privileged orders will continue to exercise their dominating influence in the very sanctuary of the Third Estate. For who has places, posts and benefices to hand out? Who needs protection and who is powerful enough to grant it? This consideration alone is enough to make every friend of the People tremble.

And the non-privileged citizens who by their abilities appear most apt to defend their order's interests, are these not reared in a superstitious or obligatory respect for the nobility? How easily most men succumb to any habit that may prove useful to them! Men are always busy improving their lot; and when self-interest cannot make progress by honest methods, it employs bad ones. Among some ancient peoples, so we read, children were trained to expect their food only after they had participated in some strenuous or skilful exercise. That was the chosen method for teaching children to excel in such matters.* In our society, the most able portion of the Third Estate has to obtain its basic needs by practising flattery and dedicating itself to the service of the powerful,

* In the First Edition, the sentence read thus: 'Some ancient people whose name I forget, trained its children to practise violent and skilful exercises by giving them their food only after they had successfully applied themselves to such efforts.'

and this kind of education is less honourable and less social but equally effective. That unhappy part of the nation has come to constitute a sort of enormous ante-room; ceaselessly noting what its masters are doing or saying, it is always ready to sacrifice everything to the fruits it anticipates from being lucky enough to find favour. When we observe such habits, how can we fail to fear that the qualities most appropriate to defend the national interest may be prostituted to defend prejudices? The boldest champions of aristocracy are to be found within the Third Estate, among the men endowed with wide intelligence but petty souls and who are as greedy for pelf, power and the caresses of the mighty as they are insensitive to the value of liberty.

Besides the empire of the aristocracy which disposes of everything in France and the feudal superstition which still further debases most minds, there remains the influence of property. Such an influence is natural and I do not condemn it; but you will agree that it is another factor that favours the privileged orders and that one can justifiably fear that it will lend them powerful support against the Third Estate. Municipalities have been too quick to believe that they could eliminate the influence of privileges by simply precluding privileged persons from representing the People. In rural areas, and indeed everywhere, any fairly popular lord who so chooses can dispose of just as large a crowd of commoners as he wants. Work out the consequences and the after-effects of this primary influence, and then remain tranquil, if you can, about their effect on an assembly which, although you picture it as far removed from the first electoral colleges, is, for all that, no more than a combination of these.[3] The more one considers this matter, the more one perceives the inadequacy of the three claims of the Third Estate.

However, even as they stand, they have been violently attacked. Let us examine the pretexts for such spiteful hostility.

First claim of the Third Estate: *That the representatives of the Third Estate be chosen solely from among citizens who really belong to the Third Estate.*

We have already explained that really to belong to the Third Estate, one must either be untainted by privileges of any sort, or else relinquish them immediately and completely.

Those lawyers who have attained nobility through a door which for unknown reasons they have decided to close behind them[1] are determined to sit in the States-General. They tell themselves: 'The nobility does not want us and we for our part do not want the Third Estate. If only we could form a separate order, it would be wonderful; however, we cannot. What are we to do? Our only chance to is maintain the old abuse by which the Third Estate elected nobles. By doing this, we shall fulfil our desires without lowering our pretensions.' All new nobles, whatever their origin, hastened to repeat in the same spirit that the Third Estate must be allowed to elect noblemen. The old nobility, which claims to be the true one, has not the same stake in maintaining the old abuse; but it knows how to take things into account. It thought: 'We shall put our sons in the *House of Commons*, so that it is altogether an excellent idea to charge us with representing the Third Estate.'

Once one has made up one's mind, reasons for it, as we well know, are never wanting. 'We must maintain the ancient *custom*,' people said. An excellent custom which, intended to provide representation for the Third Estate, has positively excluded it from representation until this very day! The Third Estate has political rights as it has civil rights; and it alone must be able to exercise both.'" What an idea—to *distinguish* between orders when it is to the advantage of the first two and the misfortune of the third, but to fuse them *together* as soon as it becomes useful to the first two and harmful to the nation! What a custom—by which the Church and the aristocracy can take over the chamber of the Third Estate! In all candour, would the privileged feel they were being represented if the Third Estate could invade the deputation of *their* orders?

In order to demonstrate the flaw in a principle, it is permissible to push its consequences as far as they can go. Using this method, I will argue thus: if the members of the three orders allowed themselves to elect whomsoever they pleased, the assembly might well end up consisting of members of a single order only. But who would admit —to take one example—that the clergy alone could represent the whole nation?

Let me go further: we have just assumed that all three estates chose their representatives from the membership of a single order. Let us now assume that the citizens all give their votes to a single individual. If this happened, is one to admit that a single individual can replace the States-General? The principle that leads to such absurd consequences is pernicious.

Another argument is that if electors are restricted in their choice they will not be completely free. I have two answers to this so-called difficulty. First, those who raise it are hypocrites, and I will prove it. Everyone knows how lords domineer over the peasants and others who live in the countryside; everyone knows the habitual and the potential tactics of their multifarious agents, including their law-officers. Hence any lord who cares to influence the primary election is generally sure to be sent as a deputy to the '*bailliage*', where it only remains to select a candidate from among the lords themselves or from those who have earned their most intimate trust. Is it then to preserve the People's freedom that you establish the possibility of abusing and betraying its trust? It is appalling to hear the sacred name of freedom profaned as a disguise for designs which are most adverse to it. Certainly, electors must be given the utmost freedom, and this is precisely why it is necessary to exclude from their deputation all the privileged classes who are too fond of overbearing the People.

My second answer is direct. In no circumstances can any freedom or right be unlimited. In all countries, the law prescribes certain qualifications without which one can be neither an elector nor eligible for election. For example, the law must decide the age under which one is incompetent to represent one's fellow-citizens. Thus, rightly or wrongly, women are everywhere excluded from mandates of this kind. It is unquestionable that tramps and beggars cannot be charged with the political confidence of nations. Would a servant, or any person under the domination of a master, or a non-naturalised foreigner, be permitted to appear among the representatives of the nation? Political liberty, therefore, has its limits, just as civil liberty has. The only question to answer is whether the non-eligibility of members of the privileged orders, which the Third Estate is asking for, is as vital as the other non-eligibilities I have just mentioned. Comparison runs completely in favour of this proposition; for the interests of a beggar or a foreigner might not conflict with the interest of the Third Estate, whereas nobles and clerics are, by their very status, supporters of the privileges which they themselves enjoy. Therefore, the restriction requested by the Third Estate is the most important of all the restrictions which the law, in accordance with equity and the nature of things, must lay down for the choice of representatives.

To emphasise this line of argument, I will make an assumption. Suppose that France is at war with England and that everything concerned with the hostilities is, at home, under the command of a Directory composed of national representatives. In such a case, I ask, would the provinces be allowed, on the pretext of not infringing their liberty, to choose members of the English cabinet as their deputies to the Directory? Yet the privileged classes are no less the enemies of the common order than are the English of the French in times of war. From among the illustrations which

F

multiply and throng in my mind, I select another. If it were *desired to create* a general Diet of maritime nations in order to establish rules for the freedom and safety of navigation, do you believe that Genoa, Leghorn, Venice, etc., would choose their plenipotentiary ministers from among the Barbary pirates? Or do you believe that the law that would enable rich pirates to buy or bribe votes in Genoa, etc., would be a good one? I do not know whether this comparison is exaggerated, but I am satisfied that it makes clearer what I had to say; besides, I hope, as well as the next man, that since enlightenment cannot long remain ineffective, the aristocrats will cease some day to resemble the Algerian pirates of France.

In accord with these principles, we must not permit men of the Third Estate who are under the exclusive domination of members of the first two orders to be given the trust of the Commons. It is clear that their dependency makes them untrustworthy; unless they are formally excluded, the lords will not fail to use the influence which they can no longer use for themselves in favour of the men whom they control. Above all, beware, I beg you, of the multifarious agents of feudalism." It is to the odious remnants of this barbaric system that we still owe the division of France, to her misfortune, into three mutually hostile orders. All would be lost if the lackeys of feudalism came to usurp the representation of the common order. Who does not know that servants are more harsh and bold to defend their masters' interests than the masters themselves? I know that this proscription covers many people since it concerns, in particular, all officers of feudal tribunals^o and the like, but, in this instance, we must be governed by the logic of the situation.

On this point, the Dauphiné has set a great example. We must follow it and declare that all tax agents and their guarantors, all administrators and the like, are ineligible for election by the Third Estate.[4] As to those who farm lands which are owned by the first two orders, I consider them also, in their present state, as being too dependent to vote freely in favour of the common order. But may I not hope that some day the legislator will consent to be informed of the interests of agriculture, good citizenship and national prosperity and that he will at last cease to believe that harsh taxation and government are the same thing? Then he will not only permit but even encourage life-tenancies, and we will be able to consider these useful farmers as independent tenants who will then be clearly competent to defend the interests of the nation.^{p}

Some people have supposed that they reinforce the difficulty of which we have just disposed by submitting that the Third Estate does not contain enough intelligent or courageous members and so forth competent to represent it, and that it has no option but to call on the leading figures of the aristocracy. . . . So ridiculous a statement deserves no answer. Look at the *available* classes in the Third Estate; and like everyone else I call 'available' those classes where some sort of affluence enables men to receive a liberal education, to train their minds and to take an interest in public affairs. Such classes have no interest other than that of the rest of the People. Judge whether they do not contain enough citizens who are educated, honest and worthy in all respects to represent the nation properly.

But then, it is argued, what if a *'bailliage'* insists on giving the mandate of the Third Estate only to a nobleman or an ecclesiastic? What if it has trust in only such a man?

I have already stated that there can be no freedom without limits and that, of all the qualifications that could be imposed on eligibility, the qualification the Third Estate requested was the most necessary. But let us give a direct answer. Supposing that one *'bailliage'* is determined to prejudice its own interests, does it follow that it must be allowed to prejudice the interest of others? If I alone am affected by the steps taken by my agent, a man may be content with simply saying to me: 'Hard luck; but why did you make such a bad choice?' But, in the case in point, the deputies of a district are not merely the representatives of the '*bailliage*' which nominated them, they are also called upon to represent the whole body of citizens, to vote for the whole kingdom. One must therefore have a common rule and such qualifications, which, although they may displease some people, will reassure the whole of the nation against the whim of a few electors.

Second claim of the Third Estate: *That its deputies be equal in number to those of the two privileged orders.*

I cannot refrain from repeating once more that the timid inadequacy of this claim is an after-effect of times gone by. The towns of the kingdom have not given enough consideration to the progress of enlightenment or even of public opinion. They would have met with no greater difficulties by demanding two votes to one; but they might even have been hastily granted the very equality which some people are so loudly opposing to-day.

Furthermore, when we want to decide a question of this kind, we must not simply do what is only too common, and give our personal wish or our will or custom as valid reasons. It is necessary to argue from principles. Like civil rights, political rights derive from a person's capacity as a citizen. These legal rights are identical for every person, whether his property happens to be great or small. Any citizen who satisfies all the formal requirements for an elector has the right to be represented, and the extent of his representation cannot be a fraction of the extent of some other citizen's representation. The right to be represented is single and indivisible. All citizens enjoy it equally, just as they are all equally protected by the law which they have helped to make. How can one argue on the one hand, that the law is the expression of the general will, i.e. the majority, and on the other hand that ten individual wills can cancel out a thousand individual wills? Would one not thereby run the risk of permitting a minority to make the law? Which would obviously be contrary to the nature of things.

If these principles, certain though they may be, are too remote from common view, I will direct the reader's attention to a comparison which lies under his very nose. Is it not a fact that it seems fair to everybody* that the huge '*bailliage*' of Poitou should send more representatives to the States-General than the small '*bailliage*' of Gex? Why is that? Because, it is stated, the population and the contribution of Poitou are far more important than those of Gex. Thus it is admitted that there are principles according to which it is

* First Edition: 'it seems fair to everybody, except to the bishop of Nev., that . . .'

possible to determine the proportion of representatives. Should we take taxation as a basis? Although we have no exact information as to the amount of taxes paid by each order, it is obvious that the Third Estate pays more than one-half of the total.

With respect to population, everybody knows that the third order enjoys a vast numerical superiority over the first two. I have no better knowledge than anybody else as to the exact proportion; but, like anybody else, I can estimate:

1) *The Clergy*

There are 40,000 parishes including Chapels of Ease. This gives us immediately the total number of parish priests including priests in charge of Chapels of Ease .. 40,000

We can count one curate for every four parishes, on an average   10,000

There are as many Cathedrals as Dioceses; let us say that, on an average, there are 20 canons per Cathedral, including the 140 bishops and archbishops   2,800

We can assume, very roughly, that there are twice as many canons regular .. 5,600

After that, one should not assume that there are still as many ecclesiastics as there are Benefices, Abbeys, Priories and Chapels. Besides, it is common knowledge that the plurality of Benefices is not unheard of in France. Bishops and canons are at the same time abbots, priors and chaplains. To avoid counting the same people twice, I estimate at three thousand the number of Benefice holders who are not already included in the figures above 3,000

Finally, I assume that there are about three thousand ecclesiastics, in Holy orders of course, who have no Benefice of any kind

.. 3,000*

We still have to count the monks and nuns whose numbers have been diminishing faster and faster in the past thirty years. I do not believe that they could be more than 17,000 nowadays 17,000

Total number of ecclesiastics .. 81,400

2) *The Nobility*

I know only one way of estimating the numbers of this order, viz. to take the province where the number is best known and to compare it with the rest of France. The province is Brittany, and I stress, in advance, it is richer in nobility than other provinces,

* In the First Edition, this figure was 2,000, bringing the total number of ecclesiastics to only 80,400.

either because nobles do not lose caste there or because their privileges are such as to keep the families at home. There are in Brittany 1,800 noble families. Actually, I will assume that there are 2,000 because some of them do not yet come to the Estates. If you say that the average family has five members, there are in Brittany 10,000 nobles of all ages and both sexes. The total population of Brittany is 2,300,000. This figure represents one-eleventh of the total French population. Therefore, if we multiply 10,000 by 11 we obtain the maximum figure of 110,000 nobles for the whole kingdom.

Therefore, in total, there are less than 200,000 privileged individuals of the first two orders.[q] Compare their number with the 25 or 26 million inhabitants, and draw your own conclusions.[5]

Now, to reach the same solution on a basis of different but equally indisputable principles, let us bear in mind that the privileged classes are to the great body of citizens what exceptions are to the law. Any society must be governed by common laws and submitted to a common order. If exceptions are to exist, at least they ought to be rare; and they must never have the same weight and influence on the commonwealth as the common rule. It is absurd to oppose the interest of the privileged classes to the grand interest of the mass of the nation as if they were capable of counter-balancing each other. (We will explain this point at greater length in Chapter 6.) When, a few years hence, we look back on all the obstacles raised to the over-modest claim of the Third State, we shall be amazed at the inadequacy of the arguments used against it, and even more at the brazen effrontery of those who were bold enough to dig them up.

The very persons who invoke the authority of facts against the Third Estate could, if they were honest, find in those facts the guide for their own conduct. The existence of a mere handful of loyal cities was enough to constitute, under Philip the Fair, a Chamber of Commons in the States-General.

Since that day, feudal servitude has disappeared and rural areas have provided a numerous population of *new citizens*. Towns have increased in number and size. Commerce and arts have, as it were, created new classes thronging with prosperous families of educated and civic-minded citizens. Why did not this two-fold increase, so much greater than the loyal cities' ancient contribution to the nation, encourage the same authority to create two new chambers in favour of the Third Estate? Justice and sound policy alike require it.

No-one dares act so unreasonably in respect of another kind of increase that has occurred in

France, viz. the new provinces which have become united with her since the last States-General met. Nobody would dare to claim that these new provinces should have no representatives of their own over and above those who were in the States-General in 1614. But do not manufactures and the arts create new riches, new taxes and a new population just as much as territory does? Since this form of increase is easily comparable to that of territory why on earth should one refuse to accord it representatives over and above the number allotted to the States-General in 1614?

But I am trying to reason with people who are moved only by self-interest. Let us present them with an argument that might touch them more closely. Is it proper for the nobility of to-day to retain the language and attitudes which were characteristic of it in the gothic centuries? And is it proper for the Third Estate, at the end of the eighteenth century, to languish in the sad and cowardly customs of ancient servitude? If the Third Estate learns how to know itself and respect itself, the others will indeed respect it too. Reflect that the former ratio between the orders has been altered simultaneously on both sides. The Third Estate, which had been reduced to nothing, has re-acquired by its industry something of what had been seized from it by the offence of those in power. Instead of demanding that its rights be restored, it has consented to pay for them; they have not been given back but sold back. But, at last, in one way or the other, it can take possession of them. It must realize that to-day it represents a reality within the nation, whereas formerly it represented only a shadow; that, while this long transformation was taking place, the nobility has ceased to be a monstrous feudal power free to oppress as it willed; that now it is the nobility that is a shadow, and that this shadow is still trying to spread terror through a whole nation— but to no avail, unless our nation is willing to be thought the basest in the world.

Third and last claim of the Third Estate: *That the States-General vote, not by orders, but by heads*.

One can regard this question from three points of view: as apprehended by the Third Estate; as relating to the interests of the privileged classes; and in terms of sound principles. As far as the first of these is concerned, it would be pointless to add anything to what we have already said; clearly, the Third Estate considers that this claim is the necessary consequence of the two others.

The privileged classes fear the third order's possession of an influence equal to their own, and so declare it unconstitutional. This behaviour is all the more striking as they have, until this moment, enjoyed a superiority of two against one without seeing anything unconstitutional in this unjust predominance. They feel passionately that they must retain a veto on everything that might conflict with their interests. I am not going to re-state the arguments by which a score of writers have combated this pretension, and the argument of 'the ancient procedures'. I want to make one observation only. There are, beyond any doubt, abuses in France; these abuses are profit-able to some persons: but they hardly ever benefit the Third Estate, and, on the contrary, it is to the Third Estate that they do most harm. Now I ask: in such circumstances is it possible to abolish any abuse so long as those who profit therefrom re-tain a veto? Justice would be powerless—every-thing would depend entirely upon the magnani-mity of the privileged classes. Would this corres-pond to our idea of what constitutes social order?

If we now turn to considering this question apart from any individual interest, but according to the principles appropriate to illuminate it, i.e. the principles of the science of social order,* it strikes us in a new light. I maintain that it is im-possible to accept the claim of the Third Estate or to defend the privileged classes without turn-ing some sure and certain ideas upside down.

* Instead of 'the science of social order', the First Edition reads 'social science'.

Naturally, I do not accuse the loyal towns of the kingdom of intending this.[6] They simply wanted to come closer to their rights by asking for at least an equilibrium between the two influences. Moreover, they have formulated some excellent truths, for it is obvious that one order's right of *veto* over the others is likely to bring everything to a standstill in a country where interests are so conflicting. It is quite certain that unless votes are counted by heads the true majority may be set aside, which would be the supreme difficulty, since it would render legislation null and void. Such truths are indisputable. But the true question is whether the orders, as now constituted, could unite to vote by heads? No, they could not. If one relies on true principle, they cannot vote *together* at all, either by heads or by orders. Whatever the proportion arranged between them, it cannot achieve the intended aim: viz. to bind all representatives together by a *single* common will. This statement doubtless calls for elaboration and for proof. Allow me to postpone these until Chapter 6. I do not want to upset the moderate-minded, who always fret in case the truth should make its appearance at the wrong moment. I must first make them admit that, simply because of the privileged classes and nobody else, conditions are now such that it is time to come to a decision, and to proclaim what is true and just in its full strength.

CHAPTER 4

*What the Government has attempted and what the
Privileged Classes propose on behalf of the Third
Estate*

The government has not been prompted by considerations for which we need to feel gratitude,
but by its own blunders; it has become convinced
that it cannot remedy these without the willing
assistance of the nation; and it has therefore
reckoned that by offering the nation some concessions it could secure from it a blind consent to
everything. This was M. de Calonne's intention
in proposing the scheme for the Provincial
Assemblies.[7]

1) *The Provincial Assemblies*

Nobody who showed the faintest concern for
the nation's interest could fail to be struck by the

political incapacity of the Third Estate. The Minister even felt that the distinction of orders prejudiced all hope of success, and without any doubt, planned to abolish it later. At least, this is the spirit in which the first plan for the Provincial Assemblies seems to have been conceived and drafted. One does not need to read it very attentively to notice that it does not allow for the *personal* status of citizens. It deals only with their properties, i.e. their *real* status. It was as property-owner and not as priest, noble or commoner that one was to be convoked to these assemblies. These were interesting by virtue of their duties, but, far more importantly, by the way they were to be constituted; for through them a genuine national representation was established.

The plan distinguished four sorts of properties. First came the *seigneuries*. Their owners, whether nobles or commoners, ecclesiastics or laymen, were to constitute the first class. Ordinary properties, as opposed to *seigneuries*, were divided into three other classes. A more natural differentiation would have created only two classes, divided according to the kind of work carried on and to the balance of material interests; namely, country and town properties. In this last class one would have included, with the dwelling-houses, all the arts, manufactures, trades, etc. But it was probably thought that the time was not yet ripe to merge ordinary church properties within these two divisions, and so it was felt necessary to put the ordinary, i.e. non-manorial, properties of the Church in a separate class, viz. the second class. The third class contained the country properties, and the fourth the town properties.

Notice that since three of these kinds of properties could be owned indiscriminately by citizens of all three orders, three classes out of the four could have been composed indiscriminately of nobles, commoners and priests. The second class itself would have contained Knights of Malta, and even laymen, to represent hospitals, parish *manufactures*, etc.

It is natural to believe that, since public business would have been transacted in these assemblies irrespective of personal status, a community of interests between the three orders would soon have sprung up; that this would in due course have become the general interest; and that the nation would have wound up at the very point where all nations ought to begin, namely by being *one*.

A great many valuable points eluded the vaunted mind of the *Principal Minister*.[8] It was not that he was not clearly aware of the interest which he wanted to serve, but that he did not understand the real value of what he was spoiling. He reintroduced the impolitic division of personal status; and although this single change called for a completely new plan, he was content to use the old

G

one whenever it did not seem to clash with his purposes; and, afterwards, he kept expressing surprise at the numerous difficulties which arose, day after day, from the want of agreement. Above all, the nobility could not conceive how it could be expected to regenerate itself in assemblies in which genealogists had been forgotten. Its anxieties on this ground were pleasant to behold.'

Of all the mistakes made in the erection of this structure, the greatest was to start with the roof instead of with the natural foundations, namely free election by the People. However, the Minister, to make some sort of obeisance to the rights of the Third Estate, did at least announce that it would have as many representatives as the clergy and the nobility taken together. His plan is positive on that point. What became of it? The Third Estate was forced to choose its deputies from the members of the privileged classes. I know one of these assemblies where, out of 52 members, there is only one who has no privilege. This is how the cause of the Third Estate is served, even after a public announcement of the intention to do it justice.

2) *The Notables*

The *Notables* fell short of the expectations of both the Ministers.[9] Nothing could depict them more truly than M.C——'s excellent stroke of the pen: 'The King called them around him twice to consult with them in the interests of the Throne and of the Nation. What did the Notables do in 1787? They defended their privileges against the Throne. What did the Notables do in 1788? They defended their privileges against the Nation.'[10] The reason is that, instead of consulting men notable for their *privileges*, one should have consulted men notable for their enlightenment. The merest private individual would not make the same mistake if he needed advice about his own business or that of people he is genuinely concerned about.

M. Necker deluded himself. But could he foresee that the same men who had voted in favour of granting an equal number of seats to the Third Estate in the Provincial Assemblies would abandon that policy of equality in respect of the States-General? Well, however that may be, the public made no mistake. It expressed continued distaste for a plan whose outcome it foresaw and from which it expected, on the most optimistic assumptions, a dilatoriness which would injure the nation. This seems to be the right place to explain some of the motives which prompted the majority of the latest *Notables*. But why anticipate the judgment of history? It will come all too quickly for men who were placed in the most favourable circumstances, and empowered to dictate to a great nation all that was just, beautiful and good, yet preferred to prostitute this superb occasion to their miserable corporate interest and so give posterity a further example of the power of prejudice over public spirit.

The efforts of the government, it is clear, produced nothing of worth to the Third Estate.

3) *Patriotic writers of the first two orders*

It is noteworthy that the cause of the Third Estate should have been defended more eagerly and forcibly by ecclesiastical and noble writers than by the non-privileged classes themselves.

In this torpidity of the Third Estate I see nothing but the habitual silence and fear which are common among the oppressed, and it provides additional proof of how real that oppression is. Is it possible to make any serious study of the principles and purpose of society without being sickened to the very soul by the monstrous partiality of human institutions! I am not surprised that the first two orders should have produced the earliest defenders of justice and humanity; for if *ability* is the fruit of a long and dedicated application of the intellect, and if members of the Third Estate are for hundreds of reasons bound to distinguish themselves in this respect, the *com-*

prehension of civic morality will arise more frequently among those whose social position affords them a conspectus of the major inter-relationships of society and whose early ambitions are less commonly cut short. It must be admitted there are sciences which depend as much on the soul as on the mind. When the nation achieves its freedom it will remember with gratitude the patriotic writers of the first two orders who were the first to abjure archaic errors and who preferred the principles of universal justice to the murderous conspiracies of corporate interest against the interest of the nation. Until those public honours are conferred upon them, may they be pleased to accept the homage of a citizen whose soul is consumed for his country and who worships all efforts which help her rise from the rubble of feudalism!

The first two orders are unquestionably interested in reinstating the third in its rights. But let us not dissimulate; the guarantee of public liberty lies only where real power lies. We can be free only with the People and by the People.

If a consideration of such magnitude is too much for the frivolity and narrow egotism of the majority of Frenchmen, these must at least be impressed by the changes in public opinion. Day by day, the influence of reason spreads further, increasingly necessitating the restitution of the rights that have been usurped. Sooner or later, every class will have to withdraw inside the boundaries of the social contract, the contract which concerns everyone, and binds all the associates one to the other.[s] Will this result in reaping its countless advantages, or in sacrificing them to despotism? This is the real question. During the long night of feudal barbarism, it was possible to destroy the true relations between men, to turn all concepts upside down, and to corrupt all justice; but, as day dawns, so gothic absurdities must fly and the remnants of ancient ferocity collapse and disappear. This is quite certain. But shall we merely be substituting one evil for another, or will social order, in all its beauty, take the place of former chaos? Will the changes we are about to experience be the bitter fruit of a civil war, disastrous in all respects for the three orders and profitable only to ministerial power; or will they be the natural, anticipated and well-controlled consequence of a simple and just outlook, of a happy co-operation favoured by the weight of circumstances and sincerely promoted by all the classes concerned?

4) *Promise to bear taxes equally*

The Notables have formally expressed the wish that all three orders should bear similar taxes,[11] but this was not what they were asked to advise upon. They were asked how to convoke the States-General, not what should be the subject of its deliberations.[12] Therefore, we must look upon that wish just as we do upon those expressed by the peers, the *Parlement* and, finally, by so many private associations and individuals, all of whom hasten to agree to-day that the richer must pay as much as the poorer.*

We cannot dissemble: so novel a co-operation has frightened some of the public. Undoubtedly, some have said, it is good and praiseworthy to pledge oneself to submit loyally to a fair distribution of taxes once the law has so decided. But (they ask) what is the origin of so novel a zeal, of so much agreement, of so much haste on the part of the second order?[13] Was it its hope that by offering a voluntary surrender it could avoid the necessity for making it a legal act of justice? Is its excessive zeal to anticipate the work of the States-General aimed at making the latter unnecessary? I will not accuse the nobility of having told the King: 'Sire, you need the States-General only to restore your finances: well! we offer to pay as much as the Third Estate; see

* The First Edition went on: 'If taxes had been what they ought to be, i.e. voluntary contributions by the tax-payers, one feels that the Third Estate would surely have been unwilling to appear more generous than the other orders.'

whether this surplus could not deliver you from an assembly which worries us even more than it does you.' No, it is impossible to take this view.

More likely, one suspects, the nobility is trying to hoodwink the Third Estate at the price of a kind of anticipation of justice, in order to divert it from its current demands and so distract it from its need to be *something* in the States-General. The nobility seems to be saying to the Third Estate: 'What are you demanding? Do you want us to pay as much as you do? That is just and we shall do so. But let things proceed as in the past when you were nothing and we were everything and when it was so easy for us to pay only as much as we chose.' How useful it would be to the privileged classes, if, for a forced renunciation, they were able to purchase the retention of all the old abuses and the hope of even increasing them! If all that is required to strike this excellent bargain is to raise a little enthusiasm among the People, do you think that it will be difficult to beguile and even placate it, by telling it that its burden will be eased, and by pouring into its ears *words* like equality, honour, fraternity . . . ?

To this the Third Estate can retort: 'It is high time that you, like us, bore the burden of a tax which is far more useful to you than to us. You correctly foresaw that this monstrous iniquity could not last any longer. If we are free to give what we choose, we clearly cannot, must not, and will not* give any more than you. Having made up our minds on this, we are virtually unmoved by these acts of renunciation which you keep vaunting as the rarest fruit of the *generosity* and the honour of the *French Knights.*[1] Yes, you will pay; not out of generosity, however, but out of justice; not because you consent to do so, but because you have to. We expect you to submit to the common laws, not to offer a token of insulting pity for an order which you have treated mercilessly for so long. But it is for the States-General to discuss this matter; to-day's question is how to constitute it properly. If the Third Estate is not represented in the States-General, the voice of the nation will be mute in that assembly, and none of its acts will be valid. Even if you were to find ways of rectifying everything without our participation we will not allow anyone to dispose of us without our consent. A long and lamentable experience prevents us from believing in the soundness of the best of laws when this comes merely as *a gift of the strongest.*[2]

The privileged classes never tire of saying that once the orders renounce their financial exemptions all is equal between them. If all is equal,

* 'must not, and will not' did not appear in the First Edition.

what have they to fear from the demands of the Third Estate? Do they imagine that it wants to damage itself by attacking a common interest? If all is equal, why then all the efforts to stop the Third Estate emerging from its political incapacity?

But, may I ask, where is the miraculous power that insures France against the possibility of any abuse of *any sort* simply because the nobility pays its fair share of a tax? Alternatively if abuses or disorders still persist, then how can all be equal between those who profit and those who suffer from them?

All is equal indeed! Was it in a spirit of equality, forsooth! that the Third Estate was ignominiously excluded from all offices and posts of any distinction? Was it the spirit of equality that made the Third Estate pay excess taxes so as to create the enormous quantity of resources of every kind for the exclusive use of what is called the *poor nobility*?

In all dealings between a privileged man and a commoner, is it not certain that the latter has no redress against oppression, since if he is bold enough to take legal action he has to appeal to members of the privileged classes? They alone dispose of authority and is not their first reaction to regard the commoner's law-suit as insubordination?

Why are the police agents so terrified when they act against a man of the privileged classes, even when they catch him red-handed, while they maltreat a pauper who is merely a suspect?

For whose benefit are all the judicial privileges, attributions, evocations, letters-patent of suspension and the like, with which to discourage or ruin the contending party? Can the non-privileged Third Estate dispose of these?

Which class of citizens are most exposed to personal humiliations from tax agents and the petty officials of every branch of the bureaucracy? The members of the Third Estate—that is, of course, the real Third Estate, i.e. the Third Estate which enjoys no exemptions.[14]

Why do the privileged nearly always escape the penalty for the most horrible of crimes? And why is public order thus robbed of its most effective examples?

With what ridiculous and ferocious contempt do you dare to relegate the criminal of the first two orders to the third, in order, so you proclaim, to *degrade* him and, apparently, to render him, in such company, *liable* to be executed! What would you say if the legislator, before punishing some scoundrel of the Third Estate, proposed to rid his order of him by giving him letters-patent of nobility?[15]

The law lays down different penalties for the

privileged classes and for the non-privileged. It appears to take a fond interest in a noble criminal and to seek to honour him right up to the scaffold. To this abominable distinction which, fundamentally, only potential criminals could wish to retain, is linked, as we know, a sentence of attainder for the entire family of the wretch who is executed without benefit of privilege. The law is responsible for this atrocity; and you would refuse to change it! If the *duty* is the same for everybody, and if the *infraction* is the same, why should the *penalty* be different? Remember: as things now stand, whenever you punish a privileged man you honour him but punish the nation which has already suffered enough from his crime.

I put it to you: cast but the most superficial glance over society and still repeat that all will be equal from the moment the nobility renounces its financial exemptions! Some men are only sensitive about money; their senses are literally paralysed at anything connected with liberty, honour or equality before the law, in short by all social rights apart from money; they cannot conceive of people worrying about anything except one crown more or one crown less. But it is not for the vile that I am writing this book.

How justify the exclusive privilege of carrying arms, even in peace-time, irrespective of any military function and without wearing the uniform of that profession? If the privileged man arms himself to defend his life, his property and his honour, why is a man of the Third Estate any less interested in protecting his life and his property? Is he less sensitive about honour? Who would dare argue that the law is so much more vigilant on his behalf that it therefore *excuses* him from arming for self-defence?

If all is equal, why the voluminous collections of laws benefiting the nobility? Have you perchance discovered how to favour one order without damaging the others? You know full well that this discriminatory legislation turns the nobility into a race apart, born to rule, and everybody else into a nation of helots, destined to serve. Yet you dare lie to your conscience and try to bemuse the nation by clamouring that 'all is equal'."

Finally, even those laws which you think are the most general and impartial are themselves accessory to the privileges. Look at the spirit in which they are drafted; trace out their consequences. For whom do they appear to be made? For the privileged classes. Against whom? Against the nation. . . .

And so the People is to be content and to forget about all this because the nobility (forsooth!) *agrees* to pay, like the People! Future

generations are to close their eyes to the enlightenment of their day and settle down quietly
to a state of oppression which the present generation can no longer endure! But let us leave this
inexhaustible topic, it does nothing but rouse
indignation.'

All taxes peculiar to the Third Estate must be
abolished. This is indubitable. What an odd
country, where the citizens who profit most from
the commonwealth contribute least to it! Where
there are taxes which it is shameful to bear and
which the legislator himself styles 'degrading'! To
think only in terms of wholesomeness, what kind
of society is it where you *lose caste* if you work?
Where to consume is honourable but to produce
is vile? Where laborious occupations are called
base? As if anything but vice could be base, and
as if this baseness of vice, the only true one,
could be found mostly among those who work![16]

Finally, words such as '*taille*',^w '*franc-fief*',
'*ustensiles*',[17] etc., must be banned from the political
vocabulary for ever and the legislator must no
longer take a stupid pleasure in repelling the
foreigners who have been prevented from bringing their capital and skills to us by these deroga-
tory distinctions.

But whilst I can foresee this and the thousand
other advantages which a well-constituted assembly must bring to the nation, I see, as yet,

nothing that promises the Third Estate an acceptable constitution. Its claims are no nearer to being granted. The privileged classes persist in defending all their advantages. Irrespective of the number of their representatives they still want to constitute two separate chambers, i.e. they want two votes out of three, and they also insist that each chamber shall have the right of veto. An excellent way to make all reform impossible! This deadlock might suit the taste of the first two orders. But can the Third Estate get much pleasure out of it? Evidently, it is not for the Third Estate to repeat the nice witticism of the Farmer-General: 'Why change? We are so well off.'

5) *Middle course proposed by friends common to the privileged classes and to the government*

What the government fears above all other things is a deliberative procedure which, by bringing all public business to a standstill, would hold up the subventions it is waiting for.* If agreement could be reached on meeting the deficit, however, it would hardly give anything else a thought; the orders could quarrel as much as and long as they wanted. Indeed, the less progress they

---

* The First Edition read: '. . . a procedure which would kill all public business.'

make, the more the government might hope
to recover its arbitrary power. It is this idea
that underlies a proposed means of reconciliation
which is beginning to be canvassed everywhere
and which would be as helpful to the privileged
orders and the government as it would be
fatal for the Third Estate. The proposal is that
the subventions and all subjects connected with
taxation should be by individual vote; but, after
that, it is suggested that the orders should withdraw into their separate chambers as into im-
pregnable fortresses,[18] where the Commons would
debate to no avail, the privileged orders pleasure
themselves without fear, while the Minister would
remain their master. But who can believe that
the Third Estate would fall into such an obvious
trap? The vote on the subventions must be the
final debate of the States-General; this will make
it necessary to agree beforehand on a general
procedure for all the debates; and we must hope
that the procedure adopted will be one that
enables the assembly to make use of all its enlightenment and of all its wisdom.[x]

6) *It is proposed to imitate the English constitution*

Within the nobility, different interests have had
time to emerge. It is not far from being divided
into two parties. All those who belong to the

most distinguished three or four hundred families sigh for an upper chamber on the English model; their pride is sustained by the hope of ceasing to be merged with the general mass of the gentle-folk. Hence the High Nobility would gladly agree to thrusting the rest of the nobility down into the House of the Commons along with the generality of the citizens.

The Third Estate must suspect a system which aims at nothing less than filling its own chamber with people whose interest is so contrary to the common interest; of a system which would soon cause the Third Estate to revert to its old impotence, to be once again a victim of oppression. From this point of view, there is a real difference between France and England. In England, the only aristocrats who have privileges are those on whom the constitution confers part of the legislative power.ʸ All other citizens share the same interest; there are no privileges to divide them into separate orders. Therefore, if in France we want to merge the three orders into one, we must first abolish all privileges of all kinds. The nobleman and the priest must have no interest other than the common interest, and by law they must enjoy only the rights of ordinary citizens. Failing these conditions, though you may unite the three orders under the same name, they will continue to constitute three heterogeneous

H

substances unable to amalgamate. No-one can accuse me of defending the distinction between orders which I regard as the most noxious of all inventions directed against the social good. I know only one misfortune which could be worse: to merge the orders *nominally* while leaving them separated *in fact* by the maintenance of privileges. Such an action would consecrate for ever the triumph of the orders over the nation. Public welfare requires that there should be some place wherein the common interest of society is kept pure and unalloyed. On this view, which is the only sound view, the only national view, the Third Estate must never consent to the admission of several orders to a so-called House of the Commons because the idea of a Commons composed of different orders is grotesque. One may say that it is a contradiction in terms.

The Third Estate's resistance will be supported by the lesser nobility which will never agree to exchange its privileges for benefits that would accrue to somebody else. Indeed, look at the way in which the lower nobility protests against the aristocracy of the Barons in Languedoc.[19] Men generally like to reduce to equality all that is above them; they then prove themselves 'philosophers'. This word only becomes odious to them from the moment when they discover the same principle operating among their inferiors.

However, the plan of bicameralism attracts so many supporters in this country that there is real occasion for alarm. The differences which we have just mentioned are real; never will a nation sliced into orders have anything in common with a nation which is *a whole*. With such different materials, how can you hope to build in France a similar political structure to England's?

Do you propose to admit part of your first two orders to the lower chamber? First, teach us how to make a Commons of several orders. As we have just shown, the Commons cannot be anything other than a body of citizens who enjoy the same civil and political rights. It is sheer mockery to use the word otherwise, to act as if it were possible to form a Commons by making citizens with unequal civil and political privileges sit in the same room. You will never find so strange a combination in England. Furthermore, it will not take long for that portion of the nobility which is to be introduced into your so-called House of the Commons to take possession of most of the seats. The Third Estate would soon lose its real representatives, and we would go back to the former state of affairs in which the nobility was everything and the nation nothing.

To avoid such drawbacks, why not reserve the second chamber exclusively for the Third Estate? In that case you would not alter your present condition. Indeed, by uniting the two privileged orders, you simply make matters worse: this alliance strengthens them as against the common order, while it weakens all the orders collectively as against the government. And this government is well aware that, between two separated nations, it will always be called in to lay down the law.

Furthermore, I still fail to see how this new arrangement brings you any closer to the English constitution. You legitimise and consecrate the distinctiveness of the privileged order; you separate its interests from those of the nation for all time; and you perpetuate the hatred, if not indeed civil war, which destroys the tranquillity of any nation divided into those who are the privileged and those who are not. In England, things are just the reverse. There all the interests of the nation are united in the House of Commons. The Lords themselves are careful not to oppose the common interest because this is also their own interest and above all that of their brothers, their children and their whole family, who belong by right to the Commons. Yet some are bold enough to compare the Upper House of England with a chamber which in France is to unite the clergy and the nobility! However you disguise it, you cannot avoid certain evils which are an essential part of it. If it is to consist of genuine representatives of the clergy and the nobility of the whole kingdom, you will, as already stated, separate for ever the two interests and renounce all hope of establishing *one* nation. If it is to be a House of Lords, you can either fill it with deputies elected by a certain number of the most distinguished families, or, to deviate even less from your English model, you can simply make the Peerage an hereditary or at least life-term privilege. All such proposals merely serve to multiply the difficulties; they all entail a House of Commons that would be hybrid and therefore preposterous. Moreover, when it pleases the King of England to create a peer, he is not obliged to pick him from a single class of citizens; this is another difference which completely upsets our own views on nobility.

I have one last point to make; it springs naturally from the conception of an Upper House composed of hereditary or life members. Such persons certainly cannot in any way be representatives of the nation, yet they would none the less exercise its powers. Frankly, now, is it impossible to imagine circumstances in which it might prove highly awkward to summon the Commons? If so, scores of reasons could easily be found to postpone it from one date to another, until time finally became so pressing that the Upper House would be conveniently invited to give prior consent to a loan, or a law, etc. I leave the rest to the reader's imagination. It would be amusing indeed if we ended up again with that *Plenary Court*[20] to which we gave such a hostile reception not so long ago! I feel that one must be allowed to dislike a measure which could lead us to the very precipice we thought we had avoided for ever. Assuredly, we need neither a *royal* chamber, nor a *feudal* chamber.

Let me just add, before passing from this topic, that I have attacked the distinction between *chambers* only in so far as it would mean a distinction between *orders*. Separate these two ideas, and I will be the first to ask for three chambers equal on all points, each of them composed of one-third of the grand national deputation. All that would need to be added to this new scheme would be to adopt the method indicated on pages 89 and 90 of *Vues sur les Moyens d'Exécution*, etc., i.e. for decisions to be taken by simple majority of heads whenever the three chambers were in disagreement with one another.

7) *A spirit of imitation is not a fit guide for us*

We would not put so much faith in English institutions if our own political knowledge was of longer standing or more prevalent. In this respect the French nation consists of men who are either too young or too old. These two age-groups, which are so closely related in many other respects, share an inability to act otherwise than by imitation. The young try to copy; the old can but repeat. The old stick to their own ingrained habits. The young ape the practices of others. This is as far as their capacity can take them.

We should not therefore be surprised to see a nation which has only just had its eyes opened, turn towards the English constitution and accept it as a model in every detail. What we need at this moment is some able writer to enlighten us on the two following questions: Is the English constitution good in itself? If so, would it be suitable for France?[z]

I am afraid that this much vaunted masterpiece cannot survive any impartial examination which is based on the principles of the true political order. We should then recognise, perhaps, that it is much more a product of chance and circumstance than of enlightenment. Its Upper House obviously bears the marks of the Revolution of 1688. We have already made the point that it can hardly be regarded as anything but a monument to gothic superstition.

Look at the national representation! See how imperfect it is in every respect, as the English themselves admit! And yet a good representation is essential for a good legislature.

How sound is the principle which inspires the notion of dividing the legislative power into three parts, of which only one is supposed to speak in the name of the nation? If the lords and the King are not the representatives of the nation, they should have no share in legislative power; for none but the nation can will for the nation and consequently legislate for the nation. But no parts of the legislative body are competent to vote in the name of the nation unless they have received a mandate from it. Yet where is the mandate when there is no free general election?

I do not deny that the English constitution is an astonishing work for its time. Nevertheless, although people are always ready to sneer at a Frenchman who does not prostrate himself before it, I am bold enough to say that I do not find in it the simplicity of good order, but rather a framework of precautions against disorder.[aa] And since all political institutions are linked together, since every effect is in its turn the origin of a series of causes and effects which can be followed as far as the mind will carry, it is not extraordinary that good minds should have thought it very profound. Furthermore it is natural that the most complicated contraptions should precede the true advances in the social arts as in all others: and their triumph likewise will be to produce great effects by simple means.

It would be wrong to prefer the English constitution merely because it has lasted for a hundred years and seems likely to last for centuries to come. As far as human institutions are concerned, is there a single one that does not last for a very long time, however bad it is? Does not despotism last? Does it not seem endless throughout most of the world?

A better test is to look at *results*. When you compare the English with their neighbours on the Continent in this respect, it is difficult to feel that they do not possess something better. However incomplete it may be, they do at least have a constitution, whereas we have nothing at all. The difference is vast. It is not surprising that it should make itself manifest in the results. But, surely, it is a mistake to attribute all that is good in England to the power of the constitution alone.

There is an obvious example of one particular law which is better than anything in the constitution itself, viz. trial by *jury*, which is the true safeguard of individual liberty wherever in the world people want to be free. This is the only legal procedure that can protect people against the abuses of the judiciary which are so frequent and so formidable wherever one is not tried by one's own peers. Under this procedure, all that freedom demands is due precaution against any illegal orders emanating from the government. This calls for either a good constitution, which England has not, or such circumstances as will prevent the head of the executive from resorting to force in support of his own arbitrary decisions. Obviously England is the only nation which can afford not to have land forces of a size dangerous to her citizens, and is consequently the only nation able to be free without a good constitution.

This consideration should suffice to dampen our passion for imitating our neighbours. Let us rather look at our own needs; they are closer to us; they will be a better source of inspiration.* If you try to naturalise the English constitution in your own country, you will quite certainly, and with the greatest ease, secure all of its defects. The reason is that these defects will serve the purposes of the one solitary power from whom you have anything to fear. The question is—will you receive its advantages as well? This is more problematical, for in this case you have to

* The First Edition read: 'Let us rather look at our own needs and our own social relationships. This constitution which we keep envying is not good because it is English. It is good because, despite its very real defects, it offers precious advantages. If you attempt to naturalise . . .'

encounter the opposition of this power, whose purpose is to thwart you. After all, why do we think so much of this exotic constitution? Apparently, because it comes close to the principles of the good society. But if ideal models of the beautiful and the good exist to guide us, and if, moreover, we are unable to say that the ideal model of society is less well known to us now than it was to the English in 1688, how then can we disregard the true good and be satisfied with imitating its copy? Let us rise at once to the challenge of setting up ourselves as an example to the nations.

It is argued that no people has done better than the English. Even if that were so, must the products of political art at the end of the eighteenth century be no better than those of the seventeenth? The English proved equal to the enlightenment of their time; let us not prove unequal to the enlightenment of ours.* Above all, let us not be discouraged because we find nothing in history that can be adapted to our present situation. The true science of society does not date back very far. Men were building cottages for many a year before they were able to build palaces. Surely

* The First Edition read: '. . . to the enlightenment of ours. That is the best kind of imitation, the worthiest way of following in the footsteps of the good examples. Above all . . .'

it is obvious that the advance of social architecture had to be even slower; for this art, the most important of all, could obviously never expect to receive the slightest encouragement from the hands of despots and aristocrats.*

* The First Edition read: '. . . before they were able to build palaces. Social architecture had good reasons for being slower in its advance than the many arts that can perfectly well co-exist with despotism.'

CHAPTER 5

What ought to have been done? Basic principles

'In morals, nothing can replace simple and natural means. But the more time man has wasted in failures, the more he dreads the thought of beginning afresh; as if it were not always better to make a fresh start and complete the task, than to lie at the mercy of events and to depend on factitious *resources with which one would begin again and yet again, and yet accomplish nothing.'*

In every free nation, and every nation ought to be free, there is only one way of settling disputes about the constitution. One must not call upon Notables, but upon the nation itself. If we have no constitution, it must be made, and only the nation has the right to make it. If we do have a constitution, as some people obstinately maintain, and if, as they allege, it divides the National Assembly into three deputations of three orders of citizens, nobody can fail to notice, at all events, that one of these orders is protesting so vigorously that nothing can be done until its claim is decided. Now, who has the right to judge in such a matter?

A question of this nature could only seem unimportant to those who disparage just and natural methods of handling social affairs and put their trust in the factitious qualities, usually rather undesirable and devious, on which the reputations of so-called statesmen, the alleged 'leading politicians', are based. As for us, we shall not deviate from the moral rule; morality must determine all the relationships which bind men to each other, both in their private interests and in their common or social interest. Morality must point out the way for us; and, after all, only morality can do so. We must always go back to basic principles for they are more cogent than all the achievements of genius.

We shall never understand social machinery unless we examine a society as though it were an ordinary machine. It is necessary to consider each part of it separately, and then link them all together in the mind in due order, to see how they fit together and hear the general harmony that necessarily follows. We need not embark on so extensive a task here. But, since one must always be clear, and since one is not clear unless one expounds from first principles, we shall at least ask the reader to distinguish three periods in the making of a political society, and these distinctions will pave the way for such explanation as is necessary.

In the first period, we assume a fairly considerable number of isolated individuals who wish to unite; by this fact alone, they already constitute a nation: they enjoy all the rights of a nation and it only remains for them to exercise them. This first period is characterised by the activity of the *individual* wills. The association is their work; they are the origin of all power.

The second period is characterised by the action of the *common* will. The associates want to give consistency to their union; they want to fulfil its aim. They therefore discuss and agree amongst themselves on public needs and on ways of satisfying them. We see that power, then, belongs to the community. Individual wills still constitute its origin and form its essential components; but, taken separately, they would be powerless. Power exists only in the aggregate. The community needs a common will; without *singleness* of will it could not succeed in being a willing and acting body. It is certain, also, that this body has no rights other than such as derive from the common will.

But let us leap the lapse of time. The associates are now too numerous and occupy too large an area to exercise their common will easily by themselves. What do they do? They separate out whatever is necessary to attend to and satisfy public requirements; and they put a few of their number in charge of exercising this portion of the national will, that is to say this portion of power. We have now reached the third period, the period of *government by proxy*. Let us point out a few facts: 1) The community does not cast aside its right to will: this is inalienable; it can only delegate the exercise of that right. This principle is elaborated elsewhere. 2) Nor can it delegate the full exercise of it. It delegates only that portion of its total power which is needed to maintain order. In this matter, no more is surrendered than necessary. 3) Therefore, it does not rest with the body of delegates to alter the limits of the power that has been entrusted to them. Obviously such a competence would be self-contradictory.

I distinguish the third period from the second in that it is no longer the *real* common will which is in operation, but a *representative* common will. It has two ineffaceable characteristics which we must repeat. 1) This will which resides in the body of representatives is neither complete nor unlimited; it is a mere portion of the grand, common, national will. 2) The delegates do not

exercise it as a right inherent in themselves, but
as a right pertaining to other people; the common
will is confided to them in trust.

For the moment I put aside a mass of problems
which this discussion naturally gives rise to, and
go straight on. What is meant by the political
constitution of a society? And what is its exact
relationship to the nation itself?

It is impossible to create a body for any purpose
without giving it the organisation, procedures and
laws appropriate for it to fulfil its intended functions. This is called the *constitution* of this body.
Obviously, the body cannot exist without it.
Therefore, it is equally obvious that every government must have its constitution; and what is true
for the government in general is true for each of
its components. Thus the Assembly of Representatives which is entrusted with the legislative
power, i.e. the exercise of the common will,
exists only in the form which the nation has
chosen to give it. It is nothing outside the
articles of its constitution; only through its constitution can it act, conduct its proceedings and
govern.

In addition to this need to organise the government so as to permit it to exist and to act, the
nation's interest also requires that the delegated
public power shall never be able to injure those
who have delegated it. Hence, a multiplicity of

I

political safeguards have been worked into the constitution: regulations imposed on the government, failure to observe which would render the exercise of power illegal.[bb]

One senses therefore the double necessity of subjecting the government to precise procedures, both internal and external to it, to ensure both its ability to fulfil and its impotence to deviate from the purpose for which it was established.

But who will tell us for what purpose and in whose interest a constitution could have been given to the *nation* itself? The nation is prior to everything. It is the source of everything. Its will is always legal; indeed it is the law itself. Prior to and above the nation, there is only *natural* law. If we want to formulate a clear idea of that sequence of *positive* laws which can emanate exculsively from the will of the nation, the first are the *constitutional* laws. These are of two kinds: some determine the organisation and the functions of the *legislative* body; the others determine the organisation and the functions of the various *executive* bodies. These laws are called *fundamental*, not in the sense that they could become independent of the national will, but because the bodies to which they grant existence and means of action cannot modify them. Neither aspect of the constitution is the creation of the constituted power, but of the constituent power. No type of delegated power can in any way alter the conditions of its delegation. In this sense, and in this sense alone, are constitutional laws *fundamental*. Those which establish the legislative body are *founded* by the national will before any constitution has been established; they form the first stage of the constitution. Those which establish the executive bodies must similarly be the *ad hoc* product of a representative will. Thus all the parts of a government are interrelated and, in the last analysis, depend on the nation. We merely put forward this idea in passing, but it is none the less correct.

Following from this, it is easy to conceive how the laws properly so-called, i.e. the laws which protect civil rights and interpret the common interest, are the work of the legislative body composed and functioning according to the terms of its constitution. Although we mention these laws *after* the constitutional laws, they are, nevertheless, the more important, for they are the *end* to which the constitution is only the *means*. They can be divided into two groups: immediate or protective laws, and mediate or guiding laws. But this is not the place to develop this analysis.[cc]

We have seen how the constitution had its origin in the second period. Clearly this constitution relates only to the government. It would be ridiculous to suppose that the nation itself could be constricted by the procedures or the constitution to which it had subjected its mandatories. If its becoming a nation had depended upon a *positive* act, it never would have existed. The nation owes its existence to *natural* law alone. The government, on the contrary, can only be a product of *positive* law. Every attribute of the nation springs from the simple fact that it exists. No act of will on its part can give it greater or lesser rights than those it already enjoys. Even in its first period, it enjoys all the rights of a nation. In its second period, it exercises them. In its third, it appoints representative to exercise those rights which are necessary for the preservation and good order of the community. To deviate from this sequence of simple ideas is simply to fall into one absurdity after another.

The power exercised by the government has substance only in so far as it is constitutional; it is legal only in so far as it is based on the prescribed laws. The national will, on the contrary, never needs anything but its own existence to be legal. It is the source of all legality.

Not only is the nation not subject to a constitution, but it *cannot* be and it *must not* be; which is tantamount to saying that it is not.

It *cannot* be. From whom indeed could it have received positive form? Is there a prior authority which could have told a multitude of individuals:

'I put you together under such and such laws; you will form a nation on the conditions I prescribe.' We are not speaking here of brigandage or domination, but of a legitimate, that is to say voluntary and free, association.

Can it be said that a nation, by a primary act of will which is completely untrammelled by any procedure, can bind itself to express its will thereafter only in certain determined ways? In the first place, a nation can neither alienate nor waive its right to will; and whatever its decisions, it cannot lose the right to alter them as soon as its interest requires. Secondly, with whom would this nation have entered into such a contract? I see how it can *bind* its members, its mandatories, and all those who belong to it; but can it in any sense impose on itself duties towards itself? What is a contract with oneself? Since both parties are the same will, they are obviously always able to free themselves from the purported engagement.

Even if it could, a nation *must* not subject itself to the shackles of a defined procedure. That would put it in danger of losing its liberty for ever, for tyranny, under the pretext of giving the People a constitution, would only need a momentary success to bind it so closely by procedural rules that it would lose the ability to express its own will, and, consequently, to shake off the yoke of despotism. We must conceive the nations of the world as being like men living outside society or 'in a state of nature', as it is called. The exercise of their will is free and independent of any civil form. Existing only within the natural order, their will can take full effect provided it bears the *natural* characteristics of a will. The manner in which a nation exercises its will does not matter; the point is that it does exercise it; any procedure is adequate, and its will is always the supreme law. To imagine a legitimate society, we assumed that the purely natural *individual* will had enough moral power to form the association; how then can we refuse to recognise a similar power in the equally natural *common* will? A nation is always in a state of nature and, amidst so many dangers, it can never have too many possible methods of expressing its will. Let us not be afraid of repeating it: a nation is independent of any procedures; and no matter how it exercises its will, the mere fact of its doing so puts an end to positive law, because it is the source and the supreme master of positive law.

But there is even stronger proof that our principles are correct, though further arguments are really superfluous.

A nation must not and cannot identify itself with constitutional forms, for as soon as a conflict arises between different parts of that constitution, what will become of a nation organised by the very constitution that is in dispute? Mark how important it is, socially, that citizens shall be able to look to some department of the executive to provide an authoritative solution for their private litigation. In the same way, the various branches of the executive must be at liberty, in a free nation,* to appeal to the legislative body for a decision whenever they meet unforeseen difficulties. But if the legislative body itself—the very basis of the constitution—is in a state of disruption, who then will be the supreme judge? For without one, order must give way to anarchy.

How can one believe that a constituted body may itself decide on its own constitution? One or more component parts of a corporate body are of no consequence individually. Power belongs only to the whole. As soon as a part protests, the whole ceases to exist; if non-existent, then how can it pass judgement?*dd* From this it follows that the constitution of a country would cease to exist at the slightest difficulty arising between its component parts, if it were not that the nation existed independently of any rule and any constitutional form.

In the light of these explanations, we can answer the question we asked ourselves. The component

* The words 'in a free nation' did not appear in the First Edition.

parts of what you believe to be the French constitution are quite obviously at loggerheads. Whose task is it to decide? It is the nation's, independent as it necessarily is of any positive forms. Even if the nation enjoyed regular States-General, this constituted body would be incompetent to decide on a dispute concerning its own constitution. It would be a *petitio principii*, a vicious circle.

The *ordinary* representatives of a nation are charged with the exercise, under the constitution, of that portion of the common will which is necessary to maintain a good social administration. Their power is confined to governmental affairs.

Extraordinary representatives will have whatever new powers the nation chooses to give them. Since a large nation cannot physically assemble when extraordinary circumstances make this necessary, it must entrust extraordinary representatives with the necessary powers on such occasions. If it could meet and express its will before your eyes, would you dare to dispute it on the ground that it did so by one procedure rather than another? Here reality is everything, the form is nothing.

A body of extraordinary representatives takes the place of the assembly of the nation. It does not, of course, need to be in charge of the *whole* of the national will; it needs only special powers, and those only in rare cases; but it is in the same position as the nation itself in respect of *independence* from any constitutional forms. It is not necessary in this case to take many precautions to prevent abuse of power; these representatives are appointed as deputies for just one purpose, and only for a limited time. I maintain that they are not bound by the constitutional forms on which they have to decide. 1) It would be self-contradictory since these forms are in dispute; it is the task of the representatives to settle them. 2) They have nothing to do with the class of matters for which definitive forms have already been settled. 3) They are a substitute for the whole nation in the course of framing its constitution. They are as independent as the nation would be in that period. They need only to will as individuals in the state of nature would will; whatever the manner in which they were appointed as deputies, whatever their method of holding meetings or debates, and bearing in mind that they are acting on an extraordinary mandate from the people (and how could the nation that mandates them be unaware of it), their common will has the same value as the common will of the nation itself.

I am not saying that a nation cannot give the aforesaid new mandate to its ordinary representatives. Identical people can certainly take part in

different bodies and can exercise in turn, by virtue
of special mandates, functions which, given their
nature, must not be merged together. But it
remains true that an extraordinary representative
body is different from the ordinary legislature.
They are distinct authorities. The latter can move
only according to prescribed forms and conditions. The former is not subjected to any procedure whatsoever: it meets and debates as the
nation itself would do if we assumed a nation
consisting of a tiny population that wanted to
give its government a constitution. These distinctions are not idle. All the principles that we
have recited are essential to social order; social
order would be incomplete if there could arise a
single case in which it was impossible to point to
rules of conduct suitable to meet all needs.*

It is time now to come back to the title of this
chapter. *What ought to have been done* amidst all the
difficulties and disputes about the coming States-
General? Should we have convened Notables? No.
Should we have let the nation and its interests
languish? No. Should we have exercised diplomacy upon the interested parties to persuade
them all to compromise? No. We should have
resorted to the extreme measure of calling an
extraordinary representative body. It is the nation
that ought to have been consulted.

Let us answer two questions which still remain.

Where is the nation to be found? Whose function is it to consult the nation?

1) Where is the nation to be found? Where it is; in the 40,000 parishes which embrace the whole territory, all its inhabitants and every element of the commonwealth; indisputably, the nation lies there. A geographical division would have been chosen so that '*arrondissements*' of 20 to 30 parishes could easily form and elect first deputies. Along similar lines, '*arrondissements*' would have formed provinces; and the provinces would have sent to the capital authentic extraordinary representatives with special powers to decide upon the constitution of the States-General.

You object that this procedure would have entailed too much delay? Surely no more than the succession of expedients which have simply led to further confusion. Besides, it was not a question of saving time, but of adopting workable measures to achieve the aim. Had people been willing and able to stick to true principles, more could have been done for the nation in four months than the progress of enlightenment and public opinion, powerful none the less as I believe it to be, could do in half a century.

But, if the *majority* of the citizens had nominated extraordinary representatives, what would have happened, you may ask, to the distinction between the three orders? What would have become of privileges? They would have become what they deserve to be. The principles which I have just recited are certainties. Abandon the hope of having social order, or else accept these principles. The nation is always free to amend its constitution. Above all, it cannot absolve itself from the responsibility of giving certainty to a disputed constitution. Everybody agrees on that to-day; cannot you see, then, that the nation could not interfere if it were itself merely a participant in the dispute? A body subjected to constitutional forms cannot take any decision outside the scope of its constitution. It cannot give itself another one. It becomes null and void from the moment when it moves, speaks or acts in any other than the prescribed forms. Even if the States-General were already in session, it would therefore be incompetent to decide upon the constitution. Such a right belongs only to the nation which, we continue to reiterate, is independent of any procedure and any qualifications.

As is obvious, the privileged classes have good reasons for befogging the concepts and principles which relate to this matter. They are boldly prepared to-day to uphold the opposite of the views they were advocating six months ago. At that time there was a single outcry in France: we had no constitution and we asked for one to be made. To-day, we not only have a constitution but, if we are to believe the privileged classes, one which contains two excellent and unchallengeable provisions. The first is the *division* of the citizens *into orders*; the second is the *equality of influence* of each order in the formation of the national will. We have already sufficiently proved that even if both these elements were indeed comprised in our constitution, the nation would always be free to change them. It remains to examine more particularly the nature of this *equality* of influence that they seek to attribute to each order in the formation of the national will. We shall see that such an idea is impossibly absurd and that no nation could possibly include anything of the kind in its constitution.

A political society cannot be anything but the whole body of the associates. A nation cannot decide not to be the nation, or to be so only in a certain fashion: for that would be saying that it is not the nation in any other fashion. Similarly, a nation cannot decree that its common will shall cease to be its common will. It is sad to have to state facts which may appear so simple as to be silly, until one thinks of the conclusions they entail. It follows that no nation has ever been able to decree that the rights inherent in the common will, i.e. in the majority, should pass into the hands of the minority. The common will cannot destroy itself. It cannot change the nature of things, nor arrange that the opinion of the minority shall be the opinion of the majority. Clearly such a regulation would not be a legal or a moral act: it would be lunacy.

Consequently if it be claimed that under the French constitution two hundred thousand individuals out of twenty-six million citizens constitute two-thirds of the common will, only one comment is possible: it is a claim that two and two make five.

The sole elements of the common will are individual wills. One can neither deny the greatest number the right to play their part, nor decide that these ten wills are equivalent to only one while another ten wills amount to thirty. These are contradictions in terms, pure absurdities.

If for the slightest moment one loses sight of this self-evident principle that the common will is the opinion of the majority and not of the minority, there is no point in carrying on the discussion. One might just as well decide that the will of a single man is to be called the majority and that we no longer need States-General or national will at all. For, if the will of a nobleman can be worth as much as ten wills, why should not the will of a minister be worth as much as a hundred? a million? twenty-six million? On the basis of this reasoning, all the national deputies may as well be sent home and every demand of the People suppressed.

Is it necessary to insist further on the logical deduction from these principles? It is a certainty that among the national representatives, whether ordinary or extraordinary, influence must be proportionate to the number of citizens who have the *right* to be represented. If it is to accomplish its task, the representative body must always be the substitute for the nation itself. It must partake of the same *nature*, the same *proportions* and the same *rules*.

To conclude: these principles are all self-consistent and prove: a) only an extraordinary representative body can establish or amend the constitution; b) this constituent representative body must be set up without regard to the distinction between orders.

2) Whose function is it to consult the nation? If the constitution provides for a legislature, each of its component parts would have the right to consult the nation, just as litigants are always allowed to appeal to the courts; or, rather, because the interpreters of a will are obliged to consult with those who appointed them to seek explanations about their mandate or to give notice of circumstances requiring new powers. But for almost two centuries we have been without representatives—even assuming that we had them at

that time. Since we have none, who is going to take their place vis-à-vis the nation? Who is going to inform the People of the need for extraordinary representatives? This question will embarrass only those who attach to the word 'convening' the hotchpotch of English ideas. We are not talking here of the royal *prerogative*, but of the simple and natural meaning of 'convening'. This word embraces: *notice* as to the national necessity and *designation* of a common meeting place. Well then, when the preservation of the motherland harries every citizen, is time to be wasted inquiring who has the *right* to convene the assembly? Ask, rather: who has not such a right? It is the sacred *duty* of all those who can do something about it. *A fortiori*, the executive is qualified to do it; for it is in a better position than private individuals to give notice to the whole nation, to designate the place of the assembly and to sweep aside all the obstructions of corporate interests. The Prince indubitably, in so far as he is the first citizen, has a greater interest than anyone else in convoking the People. He may not be competent to decide on the constitution, but it is impossible to say that he is incompetent to bring such a decision about.

So it is not difficult to answer the question, 'what ought to have been done?'. The nation ought to have been convened, so as to send to the capital extraordinary representatives with a special mandate to frame the constitution for the ordinary National Assembly. I would have objected to such representatives having the power to sit in the ordinary assembly as well. This ordinary assembly would be operating under the constitution which they had themselves drawn up in their previous capacity; hence my fear lest, instead of confining themselves to the national interest alone, they might pay too much attention to the body of which they were about to become members. In politics, it is the mingling and confusion of powers that constantly make it impossible to establish social order anywhere in the world; by the same token, the moment it is decided to separate what ought to be distinct, the great problem of organising a human society for the general welfare of its members will be successfully solved.

Why, it may be asked, do I linger so long over *what ought to have been done*? Is not the past over and done with? To this I reply: first, that the knowledge of what ought to have been done may help us to know what must be done. Secondly, it is never unimportant to expound the correct principles of one's topic, particularly when it is so new to most minds. And, finally, the truths expounded in this chapter may conduce to a better understanding of those in the one that follows.

K

CHAPTER 6

What remains to be done. Development of certain principles

Gone is the day when the three orders were moved by the single thought of defending themselves against ministerial despotism and were ready to unite against their common enemy.[21] Today, however, the nation cannot turn circumstances to advantage or take the slightest step towards social order without the Third Estate deriving some side-benefits thereby. Despite this, when the great municipalities of the realm claimed the merest fraction of the People's political rights the sight was enough to make the pride of the first two orders rebel. Just what did these privileged orders want, these orders which in this connexion are so eager to defend their own superfluity and so quick to prevent the Third Estate from obtaining its basic needs? Did they expect the vaunted regeneration[22] to be for themselves alone? Did they want to utilise the ever-suffering People as some blind instrument with which to enhance and consecrate their own aristocracy?

What words will future generations use when they learn of the ferocity with which the second order of the state and the first order of the clergy combated every demand of the municipalities?[23] Will they be able to credit the secret conspiracies and open plotting, the fake alarms,[f] the perfidiousness of the stratagems in which the defenders of the People were ensnared? Nothing of this will be omitted from the records which patriotic authors are faithfully preparing for posterity. In them they will discover how *nobly* the magnates of France conducted themselves—despite circumstances that ought to have inspired even the most brazen egotists with some sparks of patriotism. How could princes of the reigning dynasty bring themselves to take sides in a controversy between the different orders of the nation? How could they have allowed certain despicable authors to spew forth the ridiculous and yet outrageous calumnies which cram the incredible *Mémoire* published under their name?[24]

Some people complain of the violence of one or two writers of the Third Estate. What does the attitude of an isolated individual amount to?

Nothing. The only truly authentic steps taken by the Third Estate were the petitions of the municipalities and of some of the *Pays d'Etats*. Compare those to the equally authentic steps taken by the Princes against the People, although the People had carefully refrained from attacking the Princes. How modest and moderate the first are! And how violent and profoundly unjust the second!

In vain will the Third Estate await restitution of its *political* rights and the plenitude of its *civil* rights from the consensus of the orders.* The fear of seeing abuses reformed alarms the aristocrats more than the desire for liberty inspires them. Between liberty and a few odious privileges, they have chosen the latter. The soul of the privileged has become identified with the favours of servitude. They are afraid now of the States-General for which they were lately so ardent. Everything goes well with them. They have no complaints, except for the spirit of innovation. They no longer require anything: fear has provided a constitution for them.

The Third Estate must now see the direction in which both thought and action are moving, and realise that its sole hope lies in its own intelligence and courage. Reason and justice are on its side; the least it must do is to assure itself of their full

* The First Edition said 'Corporations'.

support. No, it is too late to work for the conciliation of all parties. What sort of an agreement could one hope for between the energy of the oppressed and the rage of the oppressors? They have dared utter the word *secession*. With it they have threatened both King and People. Heavens! How fortunate it would be for the nation if so desirable a secession could be perpetuated! How easy it would be to do without the privileged! How difficult it will be to induce them to become citizens!

The aristocrats who led the attack did not realise that they were making an enormous blunder by drawing attention to certain questions. Among a people used to servitude, truth can be left to sleep; but if you attract the attention of the People, if you tell it to choose between truth and error, its mind clings to truth as naturally as healthy eyes turn towards the light. And, light, in morals, cannot spread to any extent without, willy-nilly, leading to equity; for, in morals, truths are connected to rights, because the knowledge of rights arouses consciousness of them, and the consciousness of one's rights winds up, deep in the soul, the spring of liberty which is never completely broken among Europeans. One would have to be blind not to see that our nation has happily seized upon some of these fecund principles that point the way to all that is good, just and useful. It is impossible to ignore them or simply contemplate them in sterile indifference. In these new circumstances, the oppressed classes are naturally the most impressed by the need to put things right; they have acquired most interest in reinstating Justice among men—Justice, that prime virtue, long exiled from this world. It is consequently for the Third Estate to play the leading role in the advance towards national recovery. The Third Estate must, moreover, recognise the danger that unless it improves its status it cannot simply remain as it is. The circumstances do not permit of this faint-hearted calculation. Not to go forwards is to go backwards. Unless you want to proscribe this mass of iniquitous and anti-social privileges, you must decide to recognise and justify them. Yet the blood boils at the mere thought that it is possible to give *legal recognition*, at the close of the eighteenth century, to the abominable fruits of abominable feudalism. There was an epoch, and alas a long one, when the melancholy incapacity of the Third Estate warranted the regrets and the tears of patriots. But if it became its own executioner; if, just when it was able to act, it voluntarily condemned itself to contempt and opprobrium; with what emotions, with what epithets, ought we to brand it? One may weep for the weak; but one must despise the coward. Then cast aside this vision of undiluted woe; it is quite impossible, for it assumes that twenty-five million men have touched the lowest depths of infamy.

While the aristocrats talk of their honour but pursue their self-interest, the Third Estate, i.e. the nation, will develop its virtue, for if corporate interest is egotism, national interest is virtue. It will suffer the nobles to nourish their expiring vanity on the pleasure of abusing the Third Estate with the most insulting words in the vocabulary of feudalism. The nobles will repeat such words as *commoners*, *peasants* and *villeins*, forgetting that these terms, no matter in what sense one means them, either do not describe the Third Estate as it is to-day or are common to the three orders; forgetting also that, when these words did make sense, ninety-nine per cent of their own number were unquestionably *commoners*, *peasants* and *villeins*, and that the others, necessarily, were brigands. In vain do the privileged classes close their eyes to the revolution which time and events have effected: it is real for all that. There was once a time when the Third Estate was in bondage and the nobility was everything. Now the Third Estate is everything and nobility is only a word. But under cover of this word, however, and based solely on the strength of false opinion, a new and intolerable aristocracy has established itself; and the People has every reason not to want any aristocrats.[gg]

In this situation, what remains to be done by the Third Estate if it wants to take possession of its political rights in a way that will serve the nation? There are two methods of achieving this aim.

By the first method the Third Estate must meet separately; it must not co-operate with either the nobility or the clergy and it must not vote with them either by *orders* or by *heads*. Mark the enormous discrepancy between the assembly of the Third Estate and those of the other two orders. The former represents twenty-five million people and deliberates over the interests of the nation. The other two, even if they join together, derive their powers from only about two hundred thousand individuals and consider nothing but their own privileges. It is alleged that the Third Estate cannot form the *States-General* by itself. So much the better! It will form a National Assembly.[hh25] Such important advice must be justified by showing that it is firmly based on the very essence of sound principle.

I maintain that the deputies of the clergy and of the nobility have nothing in common with national representatives, that no alliance is possible between the three orders in the States-General and that they are not only unable to vote *in common*, but neither by *orders* nor by *heads*. At the end of the third chapter, we promised to provide evidence of the truth of this statement which all well-meaning readers must be quick to publicise.

A maxim of universal law lays down that *'no default is greater than default of power'*. It is public knowledge that the nobility is not deputed by either the clergy or the Third Estate and that the clergy holds no mandate from either the nobles or the commoners. Each order is in fact a separate nation which is no more competent to interfere in the affairs of the other orders than the States-General of Holland or the Council of Venice are to vote in the debates of the English Parliament. An agent can commit only his principals and a representative can speak only for those whom he represents." If the truth of this be doubted then any recourse to first principles and to rationality must be abandoned.

It follows logically from this that it is perfectly pointless to try to determine the ratio or *proportion* in which each order should participate in the making of the general will.[26] This will cannot be *one* as long as you retain three orders and three representations. At the very most, these three assemblies could meet together to pass the same resolution, just as three allied nations can express the same wish. But they will never be *one* nation, *one* representation, *one* common will.

I am aware that these truths, undisputable as

they are, tend to stir up difficulties in a state that was not founded on the basis of reason and political fair-dealing. But what do you expect! If the house you live in still stands up, that is because it is shored up. It is kept upright by a ragged forest of crude supports, erected with no more sense of design than was necessary to prop up each bit that looked like falling down. Unless it is reconstructed, you must reconcile yourself to living from day to day (as the saying goes), worrying and fearful for the moment when it will finally crush you in its ruins. The elements of social order are all interconnected. To neglect some is to endanger the others. A disorderly start makes itself felt by its consequences. The succession of events is inevitable. Ah me! If injustice and illogicality yielded the same profit as reason and fair-dealing, what advantage would lie with the latter?

You retort that, if the Third Estate meets separately, not as one of the three so-called *General* Estates, but as the National Assembly, it will be no more competent to vote for the clergy and the nobility than are these two orders to deliberate for the People. First, recollect what we have just said, that the representatives of the Third Estate unquestionably possess the mandate of the twenty-five or twenty-six million people who compose the nation, with the exception of about two hundred thousand nobles and priests. This is quite enough to entitle them to assume the title of National Assembly. They will then find no difficulty in deliberating for the entire nation, minus a trivial two hundred thousand heads.

On this assumption, the clergy could continue to hold assemblies about the 'free donation',[27] and the nobility could select some means or other of offering its subsidy to the King; and, to prevent the arrangements of these two orders from imposing too heavy a burden on the Third Estate, the latter would open with a clear and unequivocal announcement that it would pay no tax that was not equally borne by the other two orders. It would only vote the subsidy on these terms; and though voted, it would not be collected from the People if the clergy and the nobility were seen to abstain from paying their shares on any pretext whatsoever.

In spite of appearances, such an arrangement might be as good as any other as a piecemeal method of restoring social unity to the nation. It would at least provide an immediate remedy for the danger that threatens this country. The People was bound to take fright at the sight of two privileged bodies, with perhaps a third part-privileged one, making ready under the name of States-General to decide its lot and destine it to a fate as immutable as it would be wretched. Nothing could be more proper than to dispel the anxieties of twenty-five million people; when one goes so far as to talk of a constitution, one must prove by one's principles and behaviour that one knows and respects the first elements of it.

It is an established fact that the deputies of the clergy and the nobility are not the representatives of the nation; therefore, they are incompetent to vote for the nation.

If they are nevertheless allowed to discuss matters of general interest, what will be the outcome?

1) If votes are taken by *order*, it must follow that twenty-five million citizens cannot make any decision for the general interest if this displeases a couple of hundred thousand privileged individuals; or, to put it another way, that the wills of over one hundred people are to be vetoed and nullified by the will of one person alone.

2) If votes are counted by *heads* and divided equally between privileged and non-privileged, it still remains true that the wills of two hundred thousand people can cancel those of twenty-five million, since both have an equal number of representatives. Is it not outrageous to form an assembly in such a way that it can vote in the interest of the minority? Is this not an *anti*-assembly?

In the previous chapter we demonstrated that the *common* will can be discovered only in the opinion of the majority. This lies beyond question. It follows that in France the representatives of the Third Estate are the authentic trustees of the national will. They may speak then, without error, in the name of the whole nation. For, even supposing that the privileged orders always voted unanimously together against the Third Estate, they would still be incapable of outweighing the majority of the Third Estate in votes taken when this order was deliberating. For, each deputy of the Third Estate votes—according to the figure decided upon—for about fifty thousand persons; therefore all we need is a decision that a majority shall be deemed to consist of half the votes of the Third Estate *plus* five. In this way the unanimous vote of two hundred thousand nobles and priests would be covered by these five votes, and would so become irrelevant. Notice that in this supposition I have temporarily ignored the fact that deputies of the first two orders are not the representatives of the nation. Notice also my willing admission that, as members of a genuine national assembly (though disposing of no greater influence than they have a right to), they would steadily oppose the wishes of the majority. Even in such a case, their opinion would be swallowed up in the vote of the minority.

Enough has been said on this point, therefore, to demonstrate the Third Estate's obligation to form a national assembly on its own and to justify in the name of reason and fair-play its claim to deliberate and vote for the whole nation without any exception whatsoever.

I know that such principles will be distasteful even to those members of the Third Estate who are best at defending its interests. This does not matter, provided they agree that I started from correct principles and thereafter proceeded by sound logic alone. Let us add that, if the Third Estate parts company with the first two orders, it cannot be accused of *seceding*; this rash word and the meaning that it implies must be left to those who first used it. For the majority never separates from the whole; this would be a contradiction in terms because it would imply that it separates from itself. Only the minority is in the position of refusing to submit to the will of the majority and, consequently, of seceding.

However, in showing the Third Estate the full extent of its resources, or rather its rights, it is no intention of ours to get it to push them to the limit.

I pointed out earlier that the Third Estate had two methods of obtaining its rightful place in the political order. If the first, which I have just described, seems a little too abrupt; if it is felt that the public must have time to accustom itself to liberty; if it is believed that the most obvious national rights still need, if they are disputed by even the smallest number, some kind of legal pronouncement that, so to speak, establishes them and gives them a final sanction; I am willing to concur. Let us then appeal to the tribunal of the nation which is the only competent judge in any disputes about the constitution. This is the second method open to the Third Estate.

At this point we have to recall all that was said in the previous chapter about the need to *constitute* the body of ordinary representatives as well as on the need to commit this great work to the care of an extraordinary deputation given *ad hoc* special powers.

Nobody can deny that in the coming States-General the Chamber of the Third Estate will be fully competent to convoke the kingdom in *extraordinary representation*. Therefore, it is pre-eminently the duty of the Third Estate to explain the falsity of France's constitution to the citizenry. It is its duty to expostulate that since the States-General is composed of several orders, it must necessarily be ill-organised and incapable of fulfilling its national tasks; at the same time it is its duty to demonstrate the need to provide an extraordinary deputation with special powers to determine, by clearly defined laws, the constitutional forms of the legislature.

Until then, the order of the Third Estate will suspend, not of course its preparatory proceedings, but the exercise of its actual power; it will take no definitive decisions; it will wait for the nation to pass judgement in the great contention between the three orders. Such a course, I admit, is the most straightforward, the most magnanimous, and, therefore, the best suited to the dignity of the Third Estate.

The Third Estate can therefore view itself in either of two ways. The first is to regard itself simply as *an order*; in that case, it agrees not to shake off completely the prejudices of archaic barbarism; it recognises two other orders in the state, without however attributing to them more influence than is compatible with the nature of things; and it shows all possible regard for them by consenting to doubt its own rights until the supreme arbiter has made its decision.

From the second point of view, the Third Estate is the *nation*. In this capacity, its representatives constitute the whole National Assembly and are seized of all its powers. As they alone are the trustees of the general will, they do not need to consult those who mandated them about a dispute that does not exist. If they have to ask for a constitution, it is with one accord; they are always ready to submit to the laws that the nation may please to give them, but they do not have to appeal to the nation on any problem arising out of the plurality of orders.* For them, there is only one order, which is the same as saying that there is none; since for the nation there can be only the nation.

The appointment of an *extraordinary* deputation, or at least the granting of special powers, as explained above, to settle the great problem of the constitution ahead of everything else, is therefore the true means of ending the present dissension and avoiding possible disturbances within the nation. Even if these disturbances gave no cause for alarm such a step would still be necessary because, disturbance or no disturbance, we have to know where our political rights lie and take possession of them. This will be seen to be more pressing when we realise that political rights are the sole guarantee of our civil rights and our personal freedom. I invite the reader to think this over.

This is the point at which I would end my *mémoire* on the Third Estate if I had wanted to do nothing but canvass courses of action. . . . However, my other object was to explain certain principles. I therefore take leave to pursue the interests of the Third Estate beyond this point and up to the public discussion which is likely to arise over the true *composition* of a *National Assembly*.

* In the First Edition, the paragraph ended here.

L

When the extraordinary representatives frame the constitution of the legislative body, will they continue to respect the odious and impolitic *distinction* between orders?* I do not intend to discuss either their agenda or their authority, only the laws governing the personnel of the deputations. In addition to citizens, are they to include priests and nobles in a capacity other than that of citizens? Above all, are these priests and nobles to be allowed separate and superior rights by reason of this special capacity? These are great issues on which I cannot do less than expound the true principles.†

Our first task is to obtain a clear understanding of the *object* or *aim* of the representative assembly of a nation; this *object* cannot be different from that which the nation itself would propose if it could assemble and confer in any one place.

What is the will of a nation? It is the resultant of the individual wills, just as the nation is the aggregate of the individuals that compose it. It is impossible to imagine a legitimate association whose object would not be the common security, the common liberty and, finally, the common

* The First Edition went straight on from '. . . the composition of a National Assembly.' to 'I do not intend to discuss . . .'

† The First Edition read '. . . the laws governing the personnel of the deputations.'

welfare. Of course, each private individual also has his own personal aims; he thinks: 'Protected by the common security, I shall quietly pursue my own personal plans, I shall pursue happiness in my own way, sure of coming up against no legal obstacles other than those prescribed by society for the common interest in which I have a share and with which my private interest has concluded such a useful alliance.'

But who can possibly imagine the general assembly containing a member so insane as to declare: 'You are not meeting here to deliberate on our common affairs, but to attend to the private interests of myself and a small clique I have formed with a few others here'?

To say that the associates meet to decide on matters of *common* concern, is to explain the sole motive that could induce individuals to enter into association. It expresses one of those self-evident truths which are so simple that any attempt at proof merely weakens them. The object of the assembly then, is: matters of common concern.*

For our present purposes, it is worth demonstrating how every member of a National Assembly helps, through his individual will, to shape the common will which can move in only one direction: that of the public interest.

* This last sentence did not appear in the First Edition.

First of all, let us examine this political activity or mechanism on the basis of the most advantageous hypothesis: let us assume that the public spirit is so strong that it allows only activity in the common interest to be manifested in the assembly. Prodigies of this sort have been rare in the history of this world and none of them has lasted long. Only an imperfect knowledge of mankind would lead one to associate the fate of society with the efforts of virtue. At a time when public morals are in decay, when everybody seems actuated by self-interest, it is necessary—I repeat it—that, even during such ages, the assembly of a nation should be so constituted as to insulate each personal interest it contains, and ensure that the will of its majority is always consistent with the general good. Such a result is insured if the constitution enjoys support.

Three types of interest can be discerned in a man: 1) the interest in respect of which all citizens* are alike; this demonstrates the exact extent of the common interest: 2) the interest whereby an individual allies himself to a few others; this is corporate interest: finally, 3) the interest whereby everyone stands apart, thinking of himself only; this is personal interest.

The interest whereby a man concurs with all

* The First Edition read: '. . . the interest of all men in equality.'

his co-associates is obviously the *objective* of everybody's will and that of the common assembly. Each voter may bring to the assembly his two other interests; let it be so. But the first, i.e. personal interest, is not dangerous since it is insulated. To each man his own. In its diversity lies its own cure.*

Thus the major difficulty springs from the interest by which a citizen allies himself with just a few others. This type of interest leads to conspiracy and collusion; through it anti-social schemes are plotted; through it the most formidable enemies of the People mobilise themselves. History teems with examples of such misfortunes.

It is not therefore surprising that social order inflexibly requires that no citizens must be allowed to organise themselves in *guilds*, and even insists on public officials (necessarily the only persons allowed to form a genuine *corps*) renouncing the right to sit in the legislature as long as they hold office.

In this and in no other way can the common interest be made to dominate private interests.

Only on these terms can we be satisfied of the possibility of founding human associations for the general advantage of all the associates, and,

* In the First Edition, this paragraph read: 'Personal interest must have no influence. And it has none in fact; in its diversity lies its own cure.'

consequently, understand what makes political societies legitimate.

By this route and no other can we find the solution to our problem, and understand how, *in a national assembly, private interests are bound to remain insulated, and the will of the majority always conform to the general good.*

When we reflect upon these principles, we are driven to realise that we must so plan the constitution of the representative assembly that it cannot possibly develop an *esprit de corps* of its own and so degenerate into an aristocracy. Hence the fundamental maxims, developed at sufficient length elsewhere,[ii] that the body of representatives must be renewed by one-third every year; that when deputies complete their term they must be ineligible for re-election until enough time has elapsed to allow the greatest possible number of citizens the opportunity to participate in public affairs. For how could these remain public if they could come to be regarded as the peculiar property of a limited number of families . . . ?

But when, instead of conforming to these clear and unquestionable first principles, the legislator does the very opposite; when he himself creates corporations within the nation; when he recognises all those that establish themselves; when he sanctions them with his own authority; and when finally he dares to call upon the largest, most privileged and consequently most deadly ones to share, under the name of *orders*, in the national representation; then this illustrates the evil principle at work, depraving, ruining and disordering all human relationships. To complete and consolidate the social disorder, all that remains is to give these terrifying guilds an effective preponderance over the great body of the nation; and we might accuse the legislator of having done just such a thing in France, were it not more natural to attribute most of the evils that distress this superb kingdom to the blind course of circumstance or to the ignorance and the ferocity of our predecessors.

We know the true *object* of a National Assembly. Such an assembly is not set up to regulate the private affairs of individual citizens. It only regards these in the mass and from the point of view of the *common* interest. Let us draw from this the natural consequence that the right to be *represented* is enjoyed by citizens only by virtue of the qualities they share in common, not those that differentiate them from one another.

Advantages which differentiate citizens from one another lie outside their capacity as citizens. Inequalities of wealth or ability are like inequalities of age, sex, size, colour, etc. In no way do they alter the nature of the *equality* of citizenship; the rights inherent in citizenship cannot attach to differences. Of course, these *special* advantages are protected by the law; but the legislator has no right to create advantages of this kind, to give privileges to some citizens and refuse the same privileges to others. The law grants nothing. It protects what exists until what exists begins to be harmful to the common interest. These are the only limits set to personal freedom. I picture the law as being in the centre of a huge globe; all citizens, without exception, stand equidistant from it on the surface and occupy equal positions there; all are equally dependent on the law, all present it with their liberty and their property to be protected; and this is what I call the *common rights* of citizens, the rights in respect of which they are all alike. All these individuals communicate with one another, transact business, enter into contracts together, always under the common guarantee of the law. If, in this general movement, somebody wishes to rule over the person of his neighbour or usurp his neighbour's property, the common law puts down such an outrage; but it does not prevent anyone, according to his natural or acquired capacities, according to more or less favourable accidents, from increasing his property with all that a prosperous fortune or a more productive labour can add to it, nor from being able, without *expanding beyond* his legal position, to rise or to create for himself the type of happiness most suited to his taste and most worthy of envy. The law, by protecting the common rights of every citizen, protects each citizen in all that he can become up to that point when his efforts tend to prove harmful to the rights of others.[kk]*

If I harp too long on the same ideas, it is because my time is too limited to reduce them to their most simple form; besides, in formulating concepts which are over-frequently forgotten, it is inadvisable to be too concise.

Interests whereby citizens are alike, therefore, are the only ones which they can administer in common, the only ones by which and in the name of which they can claim political rights, i.e. an active part in the making of the social law; and the only ones, consequently, which qualify a citizen *to be represented*.

It follows that if one has a right to elect deputies or to be elected oneself, it is not because one is *privileged*, but because one is a *citizen*. I reiterate that everything that pertains to the citizens, both common advantages and special advantages, provided these are not against the law, has a right to protection; but since social unity is attainable only through common characteristics, a right to legislate inheres only in the common

* The First Edition said: '. . . until that point when what he wishes to be tends to harm the common interest.'

capacity. Hence corporate interest, far from weighing with legislators, can only raise their suspicions; it will always be as opposed to the purpose of a body of representatives as it is divorced from its mission.

These principles apply still more rigorously in the case of the *privileged orders*. By privileged, I mean any man who stands outside common rights, either because he claims freedom *in every respect* from subjection to the common laws, or because he claims *exclusive* rights. We have sufficiently proved elsewhere that any privilege is by its nature unjust, hateful and opposed to the social contract. A privileged class is to the nation what special advantages are to the citizen; like them, it is *not entitled to be represented*. This understates the case: a privileged class is to the nation what *harmful* special advantages are to the citizen; the legislator fulfils his duty by suppressing them. This parallel is affected by a last difference: a special advantage, though harmful to other persons, at least benefits the man who possesses it, but a privileged class is a plague for the nation which suffers, it. Thus, to reach an exact comparison, one is obliged to consider the privileged class in a nation as one would some horrible disease eating the living flesh on the body of some unfortunate man. It needs a disguise: disguise it then under all the *honorific* distinctions that you can summon up.

Thus a privileged class is noxious, not simply because of its *esprit de corps*, but because it exists at all. The more successful it has been in obtaining favours, which necessarily run counter to the general liberty, the greater the need to bar it from the National Assembly. A privileged man *could be represented*, but only in his capacity as a citizen; but, in him, this capacity has been destroyed. He stands outside citizenship. He is the enemy of common rights. To give him the right to be represented would be a manifest contradiction in the law. The nation could only submit to it through an act of servitude, and this we refuse to assume.

When we demonstrated that a member of the executive could be neither an elector nor eligible for election, we did not, for that reason, cease to regard him as a genuine citizen; he remains one, like everyone else, by virtue of his individual rights; and the necessary and honourable functions that set him apart, far from destroying his citizenship and far from harming other people's citizenship, exist, on the contrary, to serve the rights of citizenship. If it is none the less necessary to suspend the exercise of his political rights, what can be said of those who, despising common rights, have created such a special position for themselves that they have become divorced from the nation? Or of those men whose very existence amounts to perpetual warfare against the great body of the People? There can be no argument but that such people have renounced the right to qualify as citizens, and they must be excluded from the right to be electors or to be eligible for election even more surely than any foreigner would be, since the foreigner's avowed interest might well not be opposed to yours.

Let us summarise: it is a matter of principle that all those who stand outside the common quality of citizen must have no share in political rights. The legislature of a nation can be entrusted only with care of the general interest. But if instead of some simple distinction which the law hardly notices there exist persons whose privileges make them enemies of the common order, they must be positively excluded. As long as their odious privileges last, they can be neither electors nor eligible.

I realise that such principles are going to seem *extravagant* to most readers. Truth must seem as strange to prejudice as prejudice does to truth. Everything is relative. But grant that my principles are certainties and my consequences properly deduced, and that is all I ask.

'Still,' it will be said, 'things like these are absolutely *impracticable* in these days.' That is why I do not take it upon myself to put them into practice. My own role is that of every patriotic writer: to proclaim the truth. Others will either approximate to it as their ability or circumstances allow, or deviate from it because of their dishonesty; and then we shall have to put up with what we cannot prevent. If everybody's thought ran true, the greatest changes could be effected without difficulty as soon as they held out hope of public advantage. What better can I do than help with all my power to spread the truth that paves the way? It may be badly received to begin with; but, little by little, minds accustom themselves to it, a public opinion takes shape, until at the end action is taken on principles that were at first decried as imbecilities. In respect of nearly every class of prejudice, had writers not been willing to be thought *foolish*, the world to-day would be much the less *wise*.

Everywhere I go, I meet those persons who in their moderation would like to break up the truth or proclaim it only bit by bit. I suspect their understanding when they argue in this way. They underestimate the difference between the obligations imposed on the administrator and those imposed upon the philosopher. The former progresses as best he can; and provided that he does not leave the right road, he deserves nothing but praise. But the philosopher must have opened the road to its very end. Unless he has reached it, he cannot guarantee that it really is the road that leads to this end.

If, on plea of caution, he claims to stop me whenever or however seems good to him, how can I be certain that he is a good guide? Reason has no room for blind trust.

It seems that those who prefer to utter only one word at a time really want and hope thereby to surprise and entrap the enemy. I do not want to enter into a discussion as to whether plain dealing is not always the most artful, even between private individuals; but surely, the arts of concealment and all those subtleties of behaviour that we accept as the fruit of human experience are complete idiocy in national affairs, which are conducted overtly by a host of substantial and well-informed interests. Here the true means of making headway is not to conceal from the enemy what he knows just as well as we do, but to convince the majority of the citizens that their cause is just.

It is false to suppose that if the truth is divided and fragmented, the bits and pieces can thereby be fed the more easily into the mind. Not at all! Usually what is required is a powerful jolt. Truth requires every particle of its light to produce those vivid impressions that grave it for ever on the soul and evoke a passionate *interest* for everything recognised as beautiful, useful and true. Mark that in the physical world light does not proceed from the direct ray but from reflections; in the moral world it springs from the relationships between, and the sum total of, the truths pertaining to one's topic. Short of this sum total, nobody feels sufficiently informed. And the man who thinks he has the truth is often obliged to abandon this belief as he ponders the matter more deeply.

How poor an idea must one have of the progress of reason to believe that an entire nation can remain permanently blind to its true interests and that the most beneficial truths, known only to a small handful of people, must never see the light until a clever administrator requires them to forward his efforts! First, this view is false, because it is impossible to act upon. Secondly, it is bad; for who does not know that truth can only slowly penetrate a mass as enormous as a nation? There will always be all too much time wasted. The man who is troubled by the truth must be given time to get used to it; the young who receive it eagerly must be given time to become something; and the old must be given time to be no longer anything. In short, must we wait till harvest time before we sow?

What is more, reason abhors mystery. It can work powerfully only by spreading widely. Only by striking everywhere can it strike true because that is how public opinion arises, and to public opinion must probably be attributed most of the changes that have proved beneficial to peoples.

It is the one force alone that can be of use to a free nation.

You retort that minds are not yet prepared to listen to me, that I am going to shock many people? Necessarily so! The most useful truth to proclaim is not the one which people have nearly reached or the one they are on the point of welcoming. No, it is precisely because a truth is going to upset more prejudices and more vested interests, that it proves the more necessary to spread it abroad.

Not enough attention is paid to the fact that the prejudice which needs most careful handling is the one that is mingled with sincerity; that the most dangerous vested interest to arouse is the one to which sincerity lends the full force of the feeling that justice is on its side. We must deprive the enemies of the nation of this borrowed strength. We must enlighten them, and thereby condemn them to the *debilitating* consciousness of their insincerity.

The moderate-minded persons, to whom these reflections are addressed, will cease to fear for the fate of truths which they deem premature as soon as they cease to confuse the measured and cautious conduct of the administrator—who would certainly spoil everything if he did not take opposition into account—with the freedom of the philosopher. Difficulties only serve to stimulate the philosopher. He is not called upon to exercise diplomacy. His duty is to introduce sound social principles in direct proportion to the number of minds that are corroded by feudal barbarism.

When the philosopher is driving a road, he is concerned with *errors*; to make progress he must destroy them without pity. The administrator follows in his footsteps. He meets with the *interests*, more difficult to encounter, I admit. Here a new talent is required, different from the meditations of the theorist, but, make no mistake, even more foreign to the art of certain ministers who think they are administrators simply because they are certainly not philosophers.

On the other side, it is only fair to admit that the speculations of the philosophers do not always deserve to be contemptuously relegated to the category of pure fancies. If opinion can succeed in imposing laws on the legislators themselves, then the men who can influence the shaping of this opinion are not indeed as useless or as idle as so many people who never had any influence on anything are wont to claim.

Talkers who lack ideas—and there are a few of this sort—drone on and on with nonsense about what they call the importance of practice and the uselessness or the perils of theory. Only one point need be made in reply: imagine any sequence of the most wise, useful and excellent *facts* possible.

M

Well! do you believe that there is no corresponding theoretical sequence of ideas or truths that exactly corresponds to your practical sequence of facts? If you are a rational creature, this sequence of ideas will follow you, or, to be more correct, it will precede you. What is theory, pray, but this corresponding theoretical sequence of truths which you are unable to see until they are put into *practice* but which, nevertheless, someone must have seen unless we are to assume that people had been acting without knowing what they were doing. Those who clutter conversation with the gibberish that I have just mentioned do not operate either on the practical or the theoretical plane, really. Why do they not pursue the wiser and more *practical* course of receiving enlightenment from the one, if their intelligence permits; or, at the least, deriving profit from the other by keeping quiet about what they can, privately, excuse themselves for not comprehending?

Let us now return to our theme.

One final objection is that the privileged, though they may have no right to concern the common will with their privileges, must at least enjoy the political right of representation in their capacity of citizens, like the rest of society does.

However, I have already shown that in becoming privileged they have become the actual enemies of the common interest. Consequently they cannot be charged with providing for it.

To this I would also add that they are at liberty to re-enter the real nation by purging themselves of their unjust privileges, and therefore it is by their own act that they are precluded from exercising political rights. And, finally, their true rights, which are the only ones that can be the concern of the National Assembly, are common both to them *and* the deputies of the assembly. They can therefore reassure themselves with the thought* that the deputies cannot harm these interests without injuring themselves.

It is therefore quite certain that only non-privileged members are competent to be electors to, or deputies in, the National Assembly. The will of the Third Estate will always be good for the generality of citizens; that of the privileged would always be bad for it, unless, neglecting their own interests, they were prepared to vote as simple citizens. But this is the same as voting like the Third Estate itself. Therefore the Third Estate is adequate for everything that can be hoped for from a National Assembly. It follows that the Third Estate, alone, can procure all the promised benefits of the States-General.

Perhaps you may think that in the last resort

* First Edition: 'so they can find consolation in the thought that. . . '

the privileged classes can regard themselves as a separate nation and so demand a distinct and independent representation. I myself advanced this as a tentative hypothesis. But it is inadmissible. It is anticipated in the first chapter of this book where I showed that the privileged orders never were and never could be a separate nation. They exist and can do so only at the expense of the real nation. What nation would bear such a burden willingly?

Justice and reason cannot yield to private convenience. Do not ask what is the appropriate place for a privileged class in the social order. It is like deciding on the appropriate place in the body of a sick man for a malignant tumour that torments him and drains his strength. It must be *neutralised*. The health of the body and the free play of its organs must be restored so as to prevent the formation of one of these malignancies which infect and poison the very essence of life itself.*

But the word has gone round: you are not yet fit enough to be healthy! And to this aphorism of aristocratic wisdom, you give credence, like a pack of orientals solacing themselves with fatalism. Sick as you are then, so remain!

---

* The First Edition ended at this point.

AUTHOR'S NOTES

a This book, composed during the *Notables*[28] of 1788, was published in the first days of January 1789. It can be used as a continuation of the '*Essai sur les Privilèges*'.

b About Indian castes, see *Histoire Philosophique et Politique des deux Indes*, Liv. I.

c Allow us merely to point out how utterly absurd it is to argue on the one hand that the nation is not made for the head of state and to contend on the other hand that it is made for the aristocrats.*

d I do not mention the clergy here. If you regard it as a corps charged with a public duty, it belongs to society, since any public service is part

* In the First Edition, the note went on:' . . . and to contend on the other hand that it is made for those of its members who disdain to participate in the productive labours of all other citizens and in any public duty which might prove arduous. Such a class of men imposes a heavy burden on a nation! Irrefutable evidence of this lies in the facts, in the innumerable abuses of the administration, in the discouragement, in the degradation and in the misery of twenty-five million individuals.'

of the government. When one says that the clergy is a *profession* rather than an *order*, those ecclesiastics who are still living in the eleventh century, or who affect to think so because it suits their plans, complain that they are belittled. They are wrong. It is precisely because the clergy is a profession that it amounts to something among us. If it were merely an *order*, it would have no substance. As the political and moral sciences advance, the more convincing becomes the proposition that, whatever the society, there exist only private and public activities. Nothing else exists except nonsensicalities, dangerous fancies or pernicious institutions. Thus, when I maintain that the clergy cannot be considered an order, it is not to rank it lower than the nobility. The clergy must not be regarded as an order because there must be no distinction between *orders* within the nation. If, however, such distinctions could be admitted, it would probably be better to grant such a privilege to men who can show proof of a sacerdotal election, rather than grant it to men whose pretensions have no other foundation than a certificate of baptism. For, after all, one can prevent an unintelligent or dishonest man from entering the Church, but how can one prevent him from being born?*

* In the First Edition this note reads: 'I do not mention the clergy. As I see it, it is not an order, but a profession

e Caste is the right word. It describes a class of men who although they lack functions and usefulness enjoy privileges attaching to their person by the mere fact of birth. From this, which is the correct point of view, there is only one privileged caste, viz. the nobility. It is truly a nation apart, but a bogus one which, lacking organs to keep it alive, clings to a real nation like those vegetable parasites which can live only on the sap of the plants that they impoverish and blight. The Church, the law, the army and the bureaucracy are four classes of public agents necessary everywhere. Why are they accused of *aristocratism* in France? Because the caste of the nobles has usurped all the best posts, and taken them as its hereditary property. Thus it exploits them, not in the spirit of the laws of society, but to its own profit.

f An honourable author has tried to be more precise. He stated that: 'The Third Estate is the nation *less* the clergy and the nobility.' I must

charged with a public duty. In its case, privileges are not attached to the person but to the function, and this is quite different. If idle benefices can be found in the Church, they constitute an abuse. All clerics must be employed in public teaching or in the ceremonies of the cult. One cannot be accepted as a clergyman without having survived a long series of tests, but this should not cause this *corps* to be regarded as a separate caste.'

confess that I could never have mustered the
strength to announce this great truth. Anybody
else can come along and say: 'The nobility is the
nation *less* the clergy and the Third Estate,' or
'The clergy is the nation *less* the Third Estate and
the nobility.' These surely are geometrically
demonstrated propositions. I am sorry to have to
say so; but if you intended to do more than express
a rather naïve truth; if you have already grasped
what a nation is, what its components are, how
there are only public functions and private activities, and how the Third Estate can carry out all
of these without help; if you have observed that
the help which the state does receive from the
privileged caste to carry them out is exceedingly
ruinous; if you have realised that these wretched
privileges produce all the errors and evils which
distress and will long distress the French nation;
if you know that a monarchy, like any other
political system, requires only rulers and subjects,
and that a caste, which the most stupid prejudice
allows to usurp every office and to live off its
privileges, will shortly afford nothing but despots and rebels, that it will be the worst burden
that Heaven in its wrath could ever impose on a
people, and that it will become an almost in-
destructible obstacle to any plan of return to
justice or progress towards social order; if your
mind has promptly seized upon all these truths

and scores of others which also relate to our theme: why not avow frankly that the Third Estate is everything? How could you conclude such a train of considerations by the cold corollary: 'the Third Estate is the nation *less* the clergy and the nobility'?*

g On this point, the nobility has sacrificed its ancient vanity to a better understanding of its interests. In the *Pays d'Election*, the nobility of the *bailliages* (bailiwicks)[29] felt that it was impolitic to irritate the new nobles and so make them side with the Third Estate out of spite. The *Pays d'Etats* followed this maladroit rule. Experience showed it was mistaken. Thereupon the aristocracy rectified the position and admitted all those whose nobility is *hereditary*. Consequently many people who, in the *Pays d'Etats* and in the *Provincial Assemblies*, must sit only with the Third Estate are without any difficulty included in the order of the nobility in the *bailliages* and will sit with this order in the States-General. But, still, what is the point of this distinction between the nobles who can *transfer* their nobility to their children and those who allegedly cannot? If they cannot, it concerns only their children; but there is no question of admitting to our assemblies the children to whom their father has not yet trans-

* This note did not appear in the First Edition.

ferred nobility. Our only concern is the father, and he has certainly acquired, at least for himself, by letters-patent, what you say that he has not yet acquired for his children's generation: he, *personally*, is noble; admit his *person*, then, to vote with the nobility.

h Some municipal officials, the Procurators of the Royal Court of Rennes, etc., have already given the fine example of renouncing all exemptions and privileges that distinguished them from the common People.*

It is certain that common ownership of privileges is the best way to bring the orders closer together and to prepare the most important of all laws, the law changing the orders into *a single* nation.

j I cannot help expressing surprise at seeing that noblemen are excused from balloting for militia service! Is this not to show open contempt for the only pretext for so many outmoded pretensions? What will you ask payment for, if not for *the blood shed for the King*? M.C—— has stamped this old tune with ineffaceable ridicule by his quotation: 'Was the people's blood mere water?'[30]

k By the '*Resultat du Conseil*' of December 27,[31] the second claim has been *granted* without

* The word 'common' did not appear in the First Edition.

the third being mentioned and after the first had been refused. But is it not obvious that one cannot go without the others? They constitute a whole. To destroy one is to cancel all three. We shall say later whose function it is to pronounce on any matter concerning the constitution.

l They say that they want to *better the future composition* of their *order*, and for that purpose, which leads to pride through humility since it presupposes that they used to be in *bad company*, they have taken the decision that legal offices may no longer go to any families except those which already possess them to-day. You remember what we said earlier on aristocratism thirsting for all powers.

m This principle is of the utmost importance. It will be elaborated later.

n These agents' innumerable depredations continue to desolate the countryside. It is just to say that the tail of the privileged order is as obnoxious as it is itself. The Treasury with its hundred arms does not press more heavily upon the People. Well! Is it not incredible that the aristocrats have dared to utilise all this suffering in order to insinuate that the real enemies of the People come from the Third Estate! As if the tools of feudalism, the men of all liveries and all denominations who live in dependence on the aristocracy, really belonged to the Third Estate!

It is only too true that the most dangerous enemies of the People come from these classes which are divorced from the national interest, albeit not under the name of orders, and which the privileged hire for their service. France, Holland and everywhere else provide terrifying examples of the natural coalition between the lowest class of society and the privileged orders. Let us be frank; in every country in the world, the rabble belong to the aristocracy.

° Private courts! It is difficult to imagine anything more contrary to sound policy. The jurists are the ones to thank for having salvaged as much as they could from the rubble of feudal anarchy; for having clothed this gloomy structure in a similitude of legal form, and perhaps for having set some new traps inside it. One must have an odd idea of *property* to confound public posts with it and to see, with no sensation of surprise, the sceptre of so monarchical a country broken into a thousand fragments and thieves turned into legitimate owners.* Ought one not to mark how the undefined word *property* has come to shelter what is most opposed to genuine property—for instance, the right to harm others? However long the proprietorship may have lasted, how could it justify such a confusion? Public services, obviously, ought never to become

* In the First Edition, the note ended here.

the property of a private individual or be separated from sovereign duty. Let us leave that topic, then, and discuss the obvious usurpations of *common* liberty or property. Tell me: what is a *lord*, and why are *vassals* necessary? Do these metaphysical relationships (for I am not dealing with financial or material obligations) appertain to a sound political association? There is a definite possibility that the word *property* could shelter outright thefts, thefts of the sort that cannot fall under the statute of limitations. Indeed, I suppose that, in the absence of police, if Cartouche had more solidly established himself on a highway, he would have acquired a genuine right to collect a toll? If he had had time to sell this monopoly, quite common in ancient times, to a *bona fide* purchaser, would his right have become more respectable in the hands of the purchaser? Why is restitution always considered as a less fair and more impossible action than theft? There is a third class of possessions which, although they were originally legal, can be deemed harmful to the commonwealth. It is not unreasonable that compensation should be paid in such cases but they must nevertheless be extinguished. *After* such a just and necessary political discrimination, be sure that we will all fall on our knees before the sacred name of *property*; and do not believe that the man who owns least is less interested in it than he who owns most; above all, do not believe that we attack genuine property when we discredit false property.

p When an aristocrat wants to crack a joke at what he calls the pretensions of the Third Estate, he always affects to equate this order with his harness-maker, shoe-maker, etc; he then chooses the language which he thinks most proper to inspire contempt for the men of whom he speaks. But why should the more humble activities dishonour the *order of the Third Estate* when they do not dishonour a *nation*? On the other hand, when the intention is to sow dissension within the Third Estate, no difficulty is experienced in distinguishing its different classes. Townsmen and country folk are incensed against each other; efforts are made to oppose the poor to the rich. If everything could be made public I could relate many pleasing strokes of refined hypocrisy!* In spite of all these efforts, what divides men is not a difference in occupation or wealth or ability but a difference in interests. In the present case, there are only two interests: that of the privileged, and that of the non-privileged. All classes of the Third Estate are bound together by a

* The text of the First Edition went straight from 'distinguishing its different classes' to 'In spite of all these efforts'.

common interest against the oppression of the privileged.

q I observe from the above that, by deducting monks and nuns but not convents from the total number of ecclesiastics, one can infer that we are left with about 70,000 men who are truly citizens, tax-payers and who qualify to be *electors*. In the nobility, if you remove women and children, not liable to taxation and not *electors*, there hardly remain 30 to 40,000 with the same qualifications; it follows that the clergy is, relatively to national representation, a much more sizable mass than the nobility. If I make this observation, it is precisely because it is opposed to the torrent of present prejudices. I will not bow before the idol; and when the Third Estate, swept by a blind animosity, applauds a decision by which the nobility receives twice as many representatives as the clergy, I tell the Third Estate that it consults neither reason, nor justice, nor its own interest. Will the public never be able to see otherwise than through the glass of current prejudices? What *is* the clergy? A body of agents in charge of the public services of education and worship. Change its internal administration; reform it to some extent; it still remains a necessary service in some form or other. This body is not an exclusive caste but is open to all citizens; this body is so constituted that it makes no financial calls on the state. Just calculate how much it would cost the Royal Treasury to pay only the curés, and you will be terrified at the increase of taxes entailed by the squandering of Church property. Finally, this cannot avoid being a *corps*, because it is part of the administrative hierarchy. The nobility, on the contrary, is an exclusive caste, separated from the Third Estate which it despises. It is not a corps of public civil servants; its privileges are attached to the person independently of any function; nothing can justify its existence but the right of the stronger. Whereas the clergy loses privileges every day, the nobility keeps them; indeed, it increases them. Was it not yesterday that the ordinance appeared requiring *evidence* to be produced to become a military officer, *evidence* not of ability or aptitude, but of *letters-patent of nobility*, thus excluding the Third Estate from the service![32] It seems that the *Parlements* were originally created for the express purpose of supporting and strengthening the People against the tyranny of the barons, but they have seen fit to change their role; very recently and very quietly they made the nobility a perpetual gift of all seats of assessors and presiding magistrates, etc.* Has not the

---

* The text of the First Edition went straight from 'What do I say? It increases them' to 'Has not the nobility just obtained . . .'

nobility just obtained, in the *Notables of 1787*, a ruling that precedence in the Provincial Assemblies and everywhere shall henceforth alternate between itself and the clergy; and, in getting this precedence shared, did it not effectively exclude the Third Estate from it, although the Third Estate had also been summoned by the Minister? By way of a consolation prize, the Third Estate was given the sole right to choose the President of the assembly—but from the membership of the first two orders! . . . Finally, which order is more to be feared by the Third Estate, the order which gets feebler day by day and of which, by the way, it constitutes nineteen-twentieths, or the order which, just when it seems that the privileged classes ought to move towards the common order, does the reverse and finds methods to become more and more distinct? When the curés enjoy their necessary and appropriate role among the clergy, the Third Estate will see how much more rewarding it would have been to reduce the influence of the nobility rather than that of the clergy.

r See the Minutes of the Provincial Assemblies.

s It is impossible to understand the social contract otherwise than as binding the associates together. It is a wrong and dangerous idea to consider it as a contract between a people and its government. The nation cannot enter into a

N

contract with its mandatories; it is the body that *authorises* them to exercise its powers.

' I confess my inability to agree with those who attach so much importance to the privileged classes' renunciation of their pecuniary exemptions. The Third Estate does not seem to realise that, since consent to taxes is constitutionally required from itself just as much as from the others, all it has to do is to declare that it will bear no tax that is not borne by all three orders.

Nor am I satisfied with the manner in which this renunciation (over-solicited, anyway) was made in most *bailliages*, notwithstanding the show of gratitude in the newspapers and gazettes. These state that the nobility 'reserves the sacred rights of property . . . the prerogatives attaching to it . . . and the distinctions that are essential to a monarchy'. It is surprising that the Third Estate did not retort, first, to the notion that '*the sacred rights of property must be reserved*': that the whole nation had the same interest in doing that, but that it could not see against whom the clause was directed; that if orders wanted to be considered individually, history would probably tell them which of the three had most reason to mistrust the others; and that, briefly, it can only consider as a gratuitous insult what amounts to saying: 'We will pay taxes provided that you do not steal from us.' Next: what are these '*prerogatives attaching*' to a part of the nation, which the nation has never granted? Prerogatives which one would even cease to esteem if their origin were known to be something other than the *right of the sword*. Lastly, even more incomprehensibly, where are we to find those '*distinctions essential to the monarchy*', distinctions in the absence of which, presumably, a monarchy could not exist? No distinction, to our knowledge, not even the right to travel in the King's coaches, seems to be important enough to allow it to be said that, without it, monarchy *must* cease to exist.

   [u] 'I would like somebody to show me where to find the numerous privileges which people complain that we enjoy,' said an aristocrat. 'You had better say "where they are not",' answered a friend of the People. Everything about the privileged person smacks of privilege; even the way he asks questions, which would be considered extraordinary on the part of a simple citizen; even the self-assured tone with which he raises issues, so obviously solved in the depth of his soul. But, even if all privileges were reduced to one alone, I would still find it insufferable. Do you not realise that it would multiply, just like the number of privileged persons?

   [v] However, I deal here only with the inequality of *civil* rights; in the last two chapters, I will put

forward sound views on the monstrous inequality of political rights.

^w It is proper to remark that the suppression of the *taille*[33] will be to the financial advantage of the privileged if, as seems likely, it is not replaced by anything other than a general tax. The privileged classes will pay less and here is the proof:

1. In places where the *taille* is *personal*, it is well known that, basically, the tax is paid by the land-lord only. Therefore, if you substitute for the *taille** a tax bearing equally on all properties, even on those on which *taille* is not liable to be levied to-day, you clearly relieve the mass of properties that bear the *taille* to-day of the whole proportion of the replacement tax that

* The text of the First Edition differed after the words: 'If you substitute for the *taille* . . .' It read thus:

'If you substitute for the *taille* a tax common to all properties, leased lands will obviously be relieved of the whole proportion of the new tax which bears on other properties; it follows that the rich who hope to benefit from the conversion should refrain from vaunting their own generosity. Nor can the nobility take exclusive credit for the re-establishment of a sound system in those places where the *taille* is based on real property. The weight of the announced change will bear on all the owners, whether noble or not, and its advantages will be common to all owners of rural properties whether they belong to the common or the noble order. Besides the wealthy lords have calculated correctly. . . .'

will be paid by the properties which are to-day exempt from *taille*. As leased lands pay the biggest share of *taille*, it is certain that the greatest part of the relief will be to the benefit of the whole class of these estates. And since they mostly belong to the privileged classes, I am therefore right in saying that the privileged will pay less tax. 2. In places where the *taille* is based on real property, rural properties will be relieved of all that part of the replacement tax that will fall on noble properties. This commutation will be made irrespective of the personal status of the owners. Since we do not know to which order of citizens most noble lands and most rural properties belong, we cannot apportion the special advantages or disadvantages that will accrue to the nobility from the suppression of the *taille*.

The wealthy lords have calculated correctly that the abolition of the *taille*, *franc-fief*, etc., would facilitate transfers among their vassals and increase the value of the property, and consequently that it promises them new financial benefits. It is certainly wrong that the *taille* should be levied on the farmers; but, if it were levied under another name on the landlords themselves for all the properties which they *let*, it would be a perfectly sound tax, in so far as it would discourage small-holders from abandoning the management of their property, and it would play the part of a prohibitive tax or of a fine levied on large, but idle, landlords.

 * See *Vues sur les Moyens d'Exécution, etc.*, pp. 87 to 91.

 y The Lords of the Upper Chamber do not even constitute a separate order. In England, there is only one order, the nation. The member of the House of Lords is a superior mandatory appointed by law to exercise part of the legislative power and all the higher judicial functions. He is not privileged by right of caste irrespective of public functions, for the brothers of a lord do not share the privileges of the eldest. It is true that these high functions are attached to birth, or rather to primogeniture; this is a tribute paid to the feudalism that was still so preponderant a hundred years ago; it is an institution that is both gothic and ridiculous, for if kings became hereditary to avoid the civil disturbances that their election might cause, there is no reason to be afraid of anything of the sort in nominating a mere lord.

 z Since this book first appeared, an excellent work has been published that fulfils almost completely the wish I was expressing here. It is the '*Examen du Gouvernement d'Angleterre, comparé aux Constitutions des Etats-unis*', a pamphlet of 291 pages.

aa In England the right to govern is the object of an endless struggle between the administration and the aristocrats of the opposition. The nation and the King are, virtually, no more than spectators. The King's policy always consists in taking the stronger side. The nation fears both sides equally; and so, if it is to be secure, the struggle must go on. It therefore supports the weaker side to prevent it from being completely crushed. But if the People decided not to let the management of its affairs become a prize in this gladiatorial combat, and chose to look after itself through genuine representatives, can one really believe that the importance now attributed to a *balance* of powers would not disappear with the circumstances that have created it?

bb When the constitution is simple and well-framed, safeguards are few; in the countries where it is complicated and, to be frank, ill-comprehended, safeguards multiply *ad infinitum*. They provide a subject for study. The constitution itself becomes the butt of political scientists and what ought to be the essence of it, i.e. its internal organisation, is lost to view, behind the scaffolding of mere accessories.

cc Let us only say that the best way of being misunderstood is to confound all parts of the social order under the name 'constitution'.

dd In England, it is said that the House of Commons represents the nation. This is not so. Perhaps I have already said so, in which case I repeat that if the Commons alone represented the whole of the national will, they alone would constitute the whole legislative body. The constitution having decided that they are only *one* component out of *three*, it is necessary to regard the King and the Lords as being representatives of the nation as well.

ee These principles clearly decide the issue now being raised in England between Messrs. Pitt and Fox.[34] Mr. Fox is wrong not to want the *nation* to appoint as Regent *whoever* it chooses and *however* it pleases. Where the law is silent, the nation alone can decide. Mr. Pitt is wrong to want the matter to be decided upon by Parliament. Parliament is incomplete, and indeed non-existent, since the King who is the third part of it is unable to exercise his will. The two Houses can draw up a bill, but they cannot *enact* it. I take this word in the sense that usage gives it nowadays. It is necessary therefore to ask the nation to appoint extraordinary representatives. But this will not happen. The time is ripe for a good constitution, but neither the Opposition nor the Ministry feel like having one. People cling to the rules they are used to; however vicious these may be, they prefer them to the finest social order. Have you ever known a decrepit old man find compensation for his own death in the sight of the fresh and vigorous young man who is ready to take his place? It is a law of nature that political bodies, just like all living bodies, defend themselves in an effort to hold their own, right to the very end.

ff It is really too ludicrous to see the bulk of the nobility trying to denounce as rebellion against royal authority measures which they profoundly fear to be favourable to despotism. They deny that the Third Estate has any spirit and they can only account for its courage by referring to what they call the manœuvres of the Minister himself; but they are not afraid of painting this pathetic order of the Third Estate as a collection of *rebels* against the King. What the nobles say to each other is: 'Nothing is more dangerous to freedom than the language of the Third Estate; it sounds a bit too much like asking: "Sire, do with us as you please, provided you do not let the aristocrats devour us." ' But they simultaneously tell the King: 'Look out, the People is after your throne!; it plans to overthrow the monarchy.' In such a state of mind, why should they not themselves rouse the populace, with its blind and superstitious submission to whatever impulses the aristocracy chooses to transmit to it?

They would thus provide themselves with a pretext for saying: 'Here is your precious Third Estate!' But, everywhere, honest folk will answer: 'Here are the precious aristocrats! Without an aristocracy, how easily we could become, at this very moment, the first nation of the world, that is to say, the most free and the most happy!'

[gg] '*No aristocracy*' ought to become a kind of rallying-cry for all the friends of the nation and of good order. The aristocrats will think that they can retort by crying: '*No democracy*'. But we will repeat '*No democracy*' with them and *against* them. These gentlemen do not realise that representatives are not democrats; that since real democracy is impossible amongst such a large population, it is foolish to presume it or to appear to fear it; but that false democracy, alas, is all too possible; that it resides in a caste which claims by right of birth (or some such ridiculous qualification), and independently of the mandate of the People, the *powers* that the body of the citizens would exercise in a real democracy. This false democracy, with all the ills which it trails in its wake, exists in the country which is said and is believed to be monarchical, but where a privileged caste has assigned to itself the monopoly of government, power and place. Here is the feudal democracy you have to dread, which relentlessly inculcates

false fears in order to maintain its powerful influence, which hides its inability to do good
under the name of 'Corps intermédiare'[35] and its
power to do evil under the imposing authority
of the aristocrat Montesquieu. It should be
obvious to whoever cares to think about it, that
a caste of aristocrats, even if it is flattered by
the most stupid kind of prejudice, is as opposed
to the authority of the Monarch as it is to the
interest of the People.

[hh] There are great advantages in having legislative power exercised by three bodies or chambers rather than by a single one. Yet it is highly
unreasonable to compose these three chambers of
three *orders* which are hostile to one another. The
true middle course, therefore, consists in separa-
ting into three equal parts the representatives of
the Third Estate. Arranged thus you will find a
common authority, a common interest and a
common purpose. I address this remark to those
who are fond of the idea of *a system of checks and
balances between the branches of the legislative power* and
who imagine that nothing can be better in this
respect than the English constitution. Cannot one
welcome the good without adopting the bad?
Besides, as we said earlier, the English have only
one order, or rather none at all: so that if we composed our legislative checks and balances out of

different *orders*, the system would still be (we cannot repeat this too often) infinitely more vicious than that of our neighbours. It is very important that research should take place into the principles on which legislatures should be constituted, bearing in mind that one must never derogate from the *common* interest, but, contrariwise, assure it by achieving an appropriate balance between the great forces which are its essential elements. We shall deal with this question elsewhere.

ii We must, nevertheless, beware of asking for meetings of all three orders in each '*bailliage*' for the purpose of electing all deputies in common. This scheme appears to solve our difficulty; but, I think for my part that it is extremely dangerous so long as equality of *political* rights has not been established. The Third Estate must never consent to any step by which it would be compelled to recognise and sanction the *distinction* between the orders and the absurd triumph of the minority over the overwhelming majority. This imprudent behaviour would be as harmful to its own and the national interest as it would be contrary to the most elementary rules of sound policy and arithmetic.

jj See *Vues sur les Moyens d'Exécution, etc.*, sect. III.

kk I decline to undertake to answer the windy

platitudes, sometimes ludicrous by their absurdity but always so contemptible by their intention, which petty persons continue to recite so ridiculously about the fearsome word *equality*. These malign puerilities will prove short-lived and, after their day is over, writers will feel ashamed to have used their pens to refute such feeble nonsense that the very persons who are proud of it to-day will stand amazed and will scornfully cry: 'Does this writer think we are all idiots!'

[1] Cf. G. Lefebvre, *The Coming of the French Revolution*:
'What really characterised the nobility was birth; it was impossible to become a noble, but in the eyes of everyone the true nobleman was born. It was from blood that the noble derived his superiority over the "ignoble" commoners, and hence it followed that noble status was inalienable and that an unsuitable marriage was an ineffaceable blot. The aristocratic literature that flourished in the eighteenth century, more than is generally realised, side by side with the bourgeois philosophy, set itself to fortify this racial phantasmagoria by imaginary portrayals of French social history. To the Comte de Boulainvilliers, the nobles were descendants of the early Germans who had established themselves by conquest as lords over the persons and lands of the Gallo-Romans, conceived to be unskilful in arms and timid in the face of defeat. They were a distinct race, heroic and military, made for command and insistent upon the marks of respect assured by honorific distinctions.' (*Op. cit.*, Vintage Edition, New York, 1961, pp. 10–11.)

[2] These petitions were still flowing in as Sieyès was writing.

They were a direct outcome of the declaration by the States-General of Paris, September 25, 1788, that the coming Estates General must convene according to the ancient forms of 1614. Necker sought to offset this declaration by re-convening the Notables and getting them to agree to increased representation for the Third Estate. Simultaneously the leaders of the 'national party' decided to bring pressure on the municipal authorities throughout France to flood the government with petitions demanding that the Third Estate's representation should equal that of the other two orders combined; and voting by heads instead of voting by orders. They found a model for their demands in the proceedings in Dauphiné where, from September 10–28, a consultative assembly had met at Romans to frame a constitution for the Provincial Estates. This assembly had re-convened in November 1788 to learn of the government's reactions to their proposals; whereupon Mounier, the president of that assembly, seized the opportunity to draft a letter to the King in which he demanded for the nation what had been proposed for the Estates of Dauphiné: viz. the representation of the Third Estate to be equal to that of the other two orders combined, and voting by head and not by order.

Thenceforward the 'national party' throughout the towns got the municipal authorities to draft petitions to the King demanding similar arrangements for the coming States-General. Their usual practice was to canvass the town's guilds and corporations and get them to accept these demands, and to present them to the municipal authorities (or, failing them, a town meeting) for adoption and transmission to the King. The capital town having set the example, the smaller towns tended to follow suit. Thus, after Dijon had petitioned (December 16, 1788), 16 other towns of Burgundy did likewise. The example of Rouen (November 29, 1788) was followed by 25 Norman towns. Egret quotes a gazette of the time as saying:

'It is known that the number of petitions from Provinces, towns, guilds and corporations demanding a representation for the Third Estate equal to the other two orders combined is enormous, and reputed to be more than 800, not counting those flowing in on all sides every day.' (J. Egret, *La Pré-Revolution Française*, Paris, 1962, p. 358.)

³ Sieyès is simply *assuming* that the coming States-General would be indirectly elected. He could not have known this since the Royal Letter of Convocation was not published until January 24, 1789. However, he had good reason for his assumption. The new Provincial Assemblies were indirectly elected. And, elsewhere Sieyès himself lays down a plan of indirect election for his own proposed Constituent Assembly.

⁴ For the reconstruction, in a liberal fashion, of the Provincial Estates of Dauphiné, see Note 2, p. 200 above.

⁵ Modern estimates vary. G. Lefebvre (*op. cit.*, p. 8) puts the clergy at not more than 100,000 but estimates the nobility at 400,000. But it is not clear whether this figure includes people whose nobility was simply personal. It would certainly seem so. Other estimates all tend to put the nobility at about 200,000.

⁶ Another reference to the petitions of the municipalities in the autumn of 1788 (see Note 2, p. 200). Sieyès outran most of his colleagues; he argues that their programme of 'double representation' for the Third Estate and voting by heads is logically untenable and politically dangerous.

⁷ On August 20, 1786, Calonne, Controller General of Finance, faced with a yawning deficit, memorialised the King thus: 'The only course left, the sole means for a final success in putting the finances in order, must be to revivify the entire state by reforming everything that is vicious in its constitution.'

His two chief proposals were to replace the *vingtième* by a land tax levied on all landed property without distinction; and to secure this by having the citizens assess and apportion the taxes themselves. He proposed to effect this by establishing (outside the *Pays d'Etats* which already had their representative assemblies, viz. the Provincial Estates) new representative bodies called Provincial Assemblies.

These bodies were to be elected by and consist of the landed proprietors. Each parish was to elect its own assembly; the parish assemblies would elect some of their members as delegates to a district assembly; and the district assemblies would do likewise to constitute the Provincial Assembly. There was to be no distinction between the orders: the sole qualification for electing or being elected was based on proprietorship. These Provincial Assemblies were to work under the administrative control of the Intendant and their chief task would be to apportion the new land tax.

Fearing the opposition of the *Parlements* to his proposed reforms, Calonne summoned an assembly of Notables, hoping for their support for his proposals. He failed to get it, and after increasing friction between the Notables and himself, was dismissed on April 8, 1787, and replaced by his opponent, Brienne, on May 1.

[8] The expression *Principal Minister* indicates that Sieyès is now talking of Brienne, not Calonne. Calonne's title was Controller General of Finance. Brienne also held this title, but on August 26 was made Principal Minister.

In replacing Calonne, Brienne aimed at using his credit as a former Notable to push through such parts of Calonne's plans as he approved of. His first words to the Notables were to assure them that 'he had sought to fulfil the functions of a Minister during the time he had been a Notable and would try to fulfil those of a Notable now that he was a Minister'.

Qua Notable, with his fellows, Brienne had vigorously opposed Calonne's intention to suppress the distinction of

O

orders in the new Provincial Assemblies. As Minister, he now proposed that the assemblies should be constituted by orders but with the proviso that the representation of the Third Estate should be double that of the other two orders combined. This concession was resisted by the Notables and in its final form the plan provided that the Third Estate's representation would be equal to that of the other two orders combined.

An edict establishing the assemblies was promulgated June 1787, and the regulations made under it between June 23 and September 4, 1787. However, the elections were temporarily postponed. To start the assemblies up, the Crown nominated half of their membership, and these members then proceeded to co-opt the remainder. Everywhere the nobility or the clergy provided the presidents for these assemblies; and Lefebvre states (*op. cit.*, p. 29) that of the 341 members representing the Third Estate, 63 were nobles and 100 were privileged persons—not counting the bourgeois who owned manors or lawyers who were acting as agents for lords of the manor.

[9] Note 7 has already explained how Calonne decided to convene the Notables in the hope of securing their support against the obstruction he anticipated from the *Parlements*. The Notables met on February 22, 1787. They comprised (according to the *Procès Verbal* of the Assembly of Notables, Paris, 1788) 14 prelates; 36 lay magnates; 7 Princes of the Blood; 37 magistrates of the *Parlements*; 12 Councillors of State and intendants; 12 representatives of the Provincial Estates; and 26 officers of the municipal corporations. Of the latter only three were commoners. The assembly was aristocratic and privileged in the extreme.

Calonne quarrelled with the Notables and was dismissed on April 8, 1787. His successor, Brienne, had not much greater success and dismissed the Notables on May 25,

1787. Thereupon he plunged into his long struggle with the *Parlements*, described in the chronological summary at the beginning of the volume.

Necker succeeded Brienne on August 24, 1788. His plan was to rely on the forthcoming States-General which Brienne had been forced to convene. His policy was challenged, however, by the Paris *Parlement*'s pronouncement on September 25, 1788, that the States-General must meet according to its ancient form. Necker wanted the Third Estate to have a representation equal to that of the other two orders combined. To offset the *Parlement*'s declaration he therefore re-convened the Notables, on October 5, 1788, hoping that they would advise in this sense.

As Sieyès implies, Necker had good reason to hope that they would do so; for, under Brienne, they had conceded equality of representation for the Third Estate in the Provincial Assemblies (see Note 8, p. 203). But Necker was completely deceived. Led pre-eminently by a bloc of totally intransigent prelates, magistrates of the *Parlements* and Councillors of State, the Notables rejected equal representation for the Third Estate by 111 votes to 33.

[10] 'M. C——' is A. J. J. Cerutti, author of a well-known polemic, the *Mémoire pour le Peuple Français* (1788).

[11] After rejecting the proposal to grant equal representation to the Third Estate (Note 9, p. 204) the Notables recorded their wish for complete equality between the orders in respect of public taxation (November 1788).

[12] Another reference to the second session of the Notables (that convened by Necker in October 1788). The intention was to efface the impression made by the Paris *Parlement*'s pronouncement that the coming States-General must meet according to its ancient forms and hence that no concessions were to be made to the Third Estate. Necker

explained his policy thus: 'It seemed to me absolutely necessary to offset the viewpoint expressed by the first *Parlement* of the Realm by some commanding opinion and I proposed to the King that he should consult the Notables of his kingdom on this important matter.' But Sieyès's strictures as to the competence of the assembly are exact. The summons of October 5, 1788, specified that the Notables were to reassemble 'exclusively [*uniquement*] to discuss the most regular and appropriate method of going about setting up the States-General'. (Quoted, Egret, *op. cit.*, p. 339.)

[13] The second order was the nobility. The clergy formed the first order.

[14] Many bourgeois enjoyed fiscal privileges. For instance, *taille* was not paid by such persons as university students, military officers or civil servants. Again, the only class of persons charged with the *corvée* and with balloting for military service was the peasantry.

[15] The nobility benefited by virtue of certain distinctions which, in this and the following paragraphs, Sieyès holds up to ridicule. For instance, the noble enjoyed title, rank and certain honours such as the right to appear at Court. He also enjoyed certain judicial exemptions, e.g. the right to be adjudged by his peers in the *Parlement*; also, certain financial exemptions such as exemption from the duty to pay the *taille*. Within his manor he enjoyed rights of jurisdiction and to a limited extent certain financial rights. And he enjoyed the privilege of bearing arms.

On the other hand he had certain obligations. If condemned for a crime he lost his nobility '*par déchéance*'. If he lived 'ignobly' he might lose his nobility '*par dérogeance*'; and ignobly could mean (there were many local variations) simply plying a trade. For Sieyès such 'obligations' were, understandably, even more insulting to the Third Estate than the privileges and exemptions.

[16] As already noted in Note 15, if the noble ceased to live 'nobly' he lost his nobility by '*dérogeance*'. But the rule varied from district to district. In Normandy, nobility lapsed if the noble no longer had enough money to support his rank, but in other places the '*dérogeance*' was temporary. The noble entered commerce, made his fortune and then supplicated the King to have his '*dérogeance*' cancelled. Again, certain trades and vocations were open to the nobility, e.g. overseas trading, wholesaling, iron- and glass-manufacturing.

[17] For *taille*, see Note 33, p. 213 below. The *franc-fief* was a tax which a commoner had to pay on his purchasing a fief, i.e. a manor. *Ustensiles* was the duty to billet troops in passage and was usually commuted for a cash payment.

[18] This was Necker's view. (Cf. Lefebvre, *op. cit.*, p. 50.)

[19] Languedoc was one of the *Pays d'Etats*. At this moment it was in turmoil over proposals to reform its ancient Provincial Estates. While the bourgeois protested at being represented by newly created nobles and by municipal officers, the lesser nobility protested at the rule that the only nobles entitled to sit in the delegation of the order of nobility were those who possessed baronies.

[20] There were two main institutional checks on the despotism of the French monarchy in the eighteenth century. One consisted of the ancient Provincial Estates in those provinces (*Pays d'Etats*) where they still persisted. The other consisted of the *Parlements*.

These *Parlements* were courts of law of great antiquity. As judicial bodies they served mainly as courts of appeal from inferior courts; but they also possessed certain administrative functions, viz. the right to 'register' royal edicts and decrees. They had successfully expanded this right into a right to 'verify' whether such edicts were in accord with the 'fundamental laws of the kingdom' and, if they thought they were not, to remonstrate against them and even refuse registration. The King's response would then be to order the registration in a *lit de justice* at which he was personally present and, if the *Parlement* refused to acknowledge the validity of his action, to break their resistance by exiling them to some remote place by issuing *lettres de cachet*.

These *Parlements*, of which there were thirteen, were nests of aristocratic privilege. Magistrates became ennobled on acquiring their post and this nobility was hereditary. Thus was formed the *noblesse de robe*, which enjoyed the fiscal privileges common to all the nobility. Recruitment to the *Parlement* was by hereditary descent or by co-option. By this time many *Parlements* were openly fighting against the admission of commoners and some, e.g. those of Rennes, Rouen and Grenoble, refused to admit any person who could not prove four generations of nobility.

Throughout the eighteenth century, the *Parlements* had fought a running battle with the monarchy. They had defeated the reforming efforts of Machault, of Turgot and of Necker. In 1771, Louis XV had abolished them, at the hand of his celebrated Minister Maupéou; but the youthful Louis XVI had restored them. It was the conviction that these courts would obstruct his efforts at reform that led Calonne to seek to by-pass them by convening the Notables in February 1787.

As already explained in the chronological summary, Calonne and his successor, Brienne, failed to get the Notables' support and Brienne was compelled to take his proposed reforms to the Paris *Parlement*, thereupon provoking the clash of Crown *versus Parlement*. Finally, on May 8, Brienne attempted to repeat the famous '*coup de Maupéou*'.

He enforced the registration of decrees which abrogated the *Parlement*'s right to register and verify those decrees and edicts which applied to the whole kingdom. Henceforth this right was to inhere in a *Cour Plénière*. This would consist of the senior judges of the Paris *Parlement* and the president and one other magistrate from each of the provincial *Parlements*; of the Princes of the Blood; and, for the rest, of peers, government officials and leading representatives of the Church, the army and the bureacracy.

Brienne's *coup* was greeted by a howl of rage throughout France. The provincial *Parlements* declared their solidarity with the Paris *Parlement*. Riots broke out. In checking royal absolutism and demanding the recall of the States-General the Paris *Parlement* appeared to be acting in the interests of the nation as a whole. On July 5, Brienne gave way. He simultaneously suspended the decree creating the *Cour Plénière* and announced that the States-General would be convened. Brienne resigned on August 25, 1788, and his successor, Necker, lost no time in recalling the Paris *Parlement*, which met in Paris on September 23, 1788.

21 Up to September 25, 1788, aristocracy, clergy, *Parlements* and Provincial Estates had formed common front with the middle classes against the King and his Ministers. The Paris *Parlement*'s declaration of September 25, that the coming States-General must meet according to the ancient forms, 'completely changed the whole controversy', as Mallet du Pan observed. 'King, despotism and constitution are now minor questions. The war is between the Third Estate and the other two orders.' This judgement is one which all modern historians have accepted.

22 '*Regeneration*' had become a vogue-word at this time. Thus Louis XVI, explaining his decision, July 6, 1788, to convene the States-General, spoke of 'The great enter-

prise I have undertaken for the *regeneration* of the Kingdom and the re-establishment of good order in all its parts' (Egret, *op. cit.*, p. 307). Likewise Necker, in his *apologia* (*Sur l'administration de M. Necker par lui même*, 1791), wrote of 'the great enterprise that would ensure a *general regeneration*, viz. the meeting of the States-General'. (Egret, *op. cit.*, p. 325.)

[23] Note 2 above has already described the 'demands of the municipalities'. These were flowing in at the very time the Notables were meeting, at Necker's summons, to decide on the representation of the Third Estate in the coming States-General. Sieyès is here referring to the activity in this assembly of Notables. The 'second order' is of course the nobility and the first order the clergy. Egret (*op. cit.*, pp. 340–1) has pointed out that the opposition to the increased representation of the Third Estate was led by an intransigent bloc of eleven prelates, thirty-seven magistrates of the *Parlements* and twelve Councillors of State and that this bloc easily carried the majority of the Notables with them. They were vigorously opposed by a minority of twenty-four mayors and five representatives of Provincial Estates who were there to represent the interests of the Third Estate. To them must be added seven sympathetic nobles and three clerics. Egret notes in particular that 'as a whole the high Clergy closed their ears to moderation' (*op. cit.*, p. 342).

[24] Defeated in all his efforts to get the Notables to pronounce in favour of increased representation for the Third Estate, Necker prorogued the assembly on December 12, 1788. On the same day, five Princes of the Blood, viz. the Prince de Conti, and the Counts of Artois, Condé, Bourbon and Enghien, submitted their *Mémoire au Roi*. This document repeated all the arguments used in the Notables against conceding the Third Estate a representation equal to the other two orders combined; it warned

the King against a 'system of deliberate insubordination and contempt for the laws of the state' which had been caused by the 'effervescence of opinions'; it expressed fears for the future of property rights and the inequality of wealth; and it deprecated the proposals to suppress feudal rights. It begged the King 'not to sacrifice and humiliate this brave, ancient and respected nobility which has shed so much blood for the country'; a sentiment which provoked the famous riposte of Cerutti (quoted by Sieyès at p. 181), 'I suppose the people's blood was so much water?'

The *Mémoire* concluded with the contemptuous words: 'Therefore let the Third Estate desist from its attacks on the rights of the first two orders. These rights are not less ancient than the Monarchy, and are equally as unalterable. Let the Third Estate confine itself to seeking to reduce taxation with which it may be overburdened. In such an event, the first two orders, recognising in the Third Estate citizens who are dear to them, may from generosity of mind consent to renouncing their fiscal privileges and bear the burden of public taxation in equal measure.'

[25] Which is precisely what it did on June 17, 1789. Forced to meet separately from the two privileged orders in the States-General, the Third Estate proceeded (June 10) to verify the names and powers of all deputies to the States-General, beginning with the privileged orders. The latter were invited to join in this task but the only persons to do so were a few of the lower clergy. On June 17, the Third Estate and these clerics adopted by 490 votes to 90 the title of *National Assembly*, and from this time no longer passed 'resolutions' as heretofore, but 'decrees'. Also, this assembly took to itself, without permission from the Crown, the right to recast the constitution. This claim was underlined when on July 9, 1789, the assembly changed its name once more, this time to 'Constituent Assembly'.

[26] Though the general demand of the municipalities was to make the representation of the Third Estate equal to that of the other two orders combined, certain publicists were advocating different proportions. Thus Target (*Les Etats Généraux convoquées par Louis XVI . . .*) advocated that the Third Estate should have three-fifths of the total representatives. Rabaut St. Etienne proposed that it should have five-eighths of the total (*A la nation française*). In the text Sieyès condemns all such exercises as useless, since all proceed from a false premise.

[27] The Gallican Church, represented by a periodical assembly and possessing its own administrative, judicial and financial system, was subject to none of the ordinary taxes but granted on its own authority a '*don gratuit*' or 'free donation'.

[28] This fixes the date of the writing of the pamphlet between November 6 and December 12, 1788. The latest incident referred to in the work is the *Résultat du Conseil* of December 27, 1788. The fact that this reference—despite its importance to Sieyès's general argument—occurs only in a footnote, suggests that by that date the MS. was already in the hands of the printer.

[29] The *bailliage* (bailiwick), which in some places was called a *sénéchaussée*, was the subdivision of a province for judicial and administrative purposes.

[30] i.e. A. J. J. Cerutti. This was his riposte to the *Mémoire au Roi* of December 12, 1788. (See Note 24, p. 210.)

[31] After the Notables had rejected the proposal to make the Third Estate's representation equal to that of the other two orders combined, Necker dismissed them (December 12, 1788) and took the fight to the Royal Council. There, after prolonged argument, he got his way. The decisions were recorded, not as might have been

expected by a law or decree, but by a communiqué with the laconic title: *Le Résultat du Conseil du 27 Décembre, 1788.* It ran:

1. The deputies to the forthcoming States-General will number at least one thousand.

2. This number will be made up, as far as possible, by reference to the population and the taxes paid in each *bailliage*.

3. The number of deputies of the Third Estate will be equal to that of the two other orders combined.

[32] The regulation of May 22, 1781, prescribed that youths who desired to be nominated as sub-lieutenants in the infantry and cavalry without serving in the ranks, must prove four generations of nobility on their father's side.

[33] *Taille*, the most important of the taxes, varied in form and onerousness from province to province. It took two main forms. *Taille personelle* was based on the status of the tax-payer and was paid by members of the Third Estate who had not been granted exemption from it. In practice it fell exclusively on the poor and the peasantry. *Taille réelle*, however, was based on property irrespective of the status of the owner.

[34] In November 1788, George III became insane. Thereupon his Prime Minister, Pitt, proposed that the Prince of Wales should become Regent, but under certain restrictions laid down by statute. Fox and Burke, the opposition leaders, insisted that the Prince succeeded automatically and to the full plenitude of royal power once the King's incapacity was established. They argued further that in the event of such incapacity a statute such as Pitt had proposed was an impossibility, since the necessary royal consent could not be forthcoming. From this imbroglio Parliament was suddenly rescued (February 1789) by the King's return to sanity.

[35] For Montesquieu, it was what we should to-day call the 'countervailing power' of subordinate groupings, viz. the nobility, the clergy, the *Parlements* and the municipalities, which tempered royal power and prevented despotism. These groupings he called the '*pouvoirs intermédiaires*' (cf. *L'Esprit des Lois*, Book II, Chapter 4).

The following French editions have appeared.

Qu'est ce que le Tiers Etat? 1789, octavo, 127 pages.

Qu'est ce que le Tiers Etat? 2nd edition, revised, 1789, octavo, 114 pages.

Qu'est ce que le Tiers Etat? 2nd edition, revised, 1789, octavo, 130 pages.

Qu'est ce que le Tiers Etat? 3rd edition, 1789, octavo, 180 pages.

Qu'est ce que le Tiers Etat? preceded by the *Essai sur les Privilèges*, new edition including 23 footnotes by the Abbé Morellet, Paris, Corréard, 1822, octavo, 224 pages.

Qu'est ce que le Tiers Etat? a pamphlet published in 1789 by Sieyès preceded by a study on the author by M. Chapuys-Montlaville, *député*, and illustrated with a portrait of Sieyès, Paris, Pagnerre, 1839, petit octavo, 192 pages.

Finally, *Qu'est ce que le Tiers Etat?* preceded by the *Essai sur les Privilèges, édition critique avec une introduction par Edme Champion*, 1888, Société de l'histoire de la Révolution Française, Paris, xv + 93 pages.

In *La France littéraire* by J. S. Ersch, Hamburg, 1798, 3 vols., octavo, under the heading Sieyès, the author states that the *Essai sur les Privilèges* and *Qu'est ce que le Tiers Etat?* were translated into English in 1791, in an octavo edition. But Champion, in his 1888 edition, states that he was unable to trace any such translation, and neither can we.